LOST TREASURES *of* CINCINNATI

Amy E. Brownlee

Reedy Press
PO Box 5131
St. Louis, MO 63139, USA
www.reedypress.com

Library of Congress Control Number: 2021935149

ISBN: 9781681063263

Printed in the United States of America

22 23 24 25 26 5 4 3 2 1

DEDICATION

To Tim, Joanna, and Sarah, who make this hometown a home.

TABLE OF CONTENTS

ACKNOWLEDGMENTS

Thanks to all the people who have helped me cross the finish line with this book. I can't do them all justice, but here's my very best shot:

To Greg Hand, thank you for introducing me to this series concept and then passing my name along to Reedy Press. You held a door wide open for me and gave me a shot at a professional first: writing a book. You have always been encouraging, amusing, and an all-around ray of sunshine in my inbox.

I'd also like to thank the following individuals for their help and guidance: Reedy Press editors and staffers, especially Chelcie Grant, Barbara Northcott, James Schwentker, and Josh Stevens; Cincinnati and Hamilton County Public Library staff, especially Larry Richmond, Katrina Marshall, and Kevin Welch; Dr. Eric R. Jackson; Gregg Fraley; Suzy DeYoung; Lynne Knueven; Herman "Butch" Knueven, Brian Knueven, and Anne Bangert.

And to my husband Tim Brownlee, who always waited in the car while I took another picture, who read many drafts, and who made even more suggestions: Thank you for your tireless help. I still think you're wrong about that one semi-colon, but I love you anyway.

INTRODUCTION

Union Terminal is both a champion and villain in this book. The iconic art deco train station stands today as a monument to preservation activism, civic teamwork, and a keen regional audience sustained over generations. It took time to get here—years of dithering and a slate of just terrible ideas (e.g., converting it to a shopping mall)—before Union Terminal carved out a new role in the city's culture. Named a National Historic Landmark in 1977, the station is now host to the Cincinnati Museum Center, a conglomerate of five institutions, including the Cincinnati History Museum, The Children's Museum, the Museum of Natural History & Science, the Nancy & David Wolf Holocaust & Humanity Center, and the Cincinnati History Library and Archives.

The Union Terminal's success story is a source of pride for Cincinnati. However, Union Terminal's construction left a huge footprint, and is responsible for seven entries on this *Lost Treasures* list. The construction took out proximal structures and natural areas, like Lincoln Park Baptist Church and the surrounding Lincoln Park, an urban oasis with trees, a grotto, and a lake that gave way to the station's fountain esplanade. The newly graded and spacious lawn was a fitting entrance to emphasize the scale of the building rising tall over Western Avenue, but it was a pale substitution for what it replaced. And eventually, as was the fate for far too many places in this book, much of its square footage was converted to a surface parking lot (though its scalloped, stair-step fountain blessedly remains).

Union Terminal's impact also reached throughout the city to dismantle a network of neighborhood passenger train stations like Pennsylvania Station, Cincinnati, Hamilton, & Dayton Railway Station, Torrence Road Station, and Central Union Station. These local outfits would today be luxurious markers of urban living, but in the 1930s, they were just costly clutter holding Cincinnati hostage in the previous century. The gleaming new West End train station was designed to replace them all, and represented a unified city with an eye towards progress—even at great cost. (Despite the heroic preservation of the building, Union Terminal still represents the lost culture and infrastructure of passenger rail travel in the United States, which is a worthy subject for another book.)

With all evidence to the contrary, Cincinnati is actually remarkably adept at preserving its history. Put it down to a love of local lore, or to its sluggish evolution. (Mark Twain said it best: "When the end of the world comes, I want to be in Cincinnati because it's always 20 years behind the times.") For every item listed here, there is another place still standing, still striving, still on someone's list to save.

The goal of this book is not only to bemoan what is lost to Cincinnati, though to be fair, that certainly will be part of the project of reading it. It's hard not to follow these stories and see these images without feeling a sense of loss. It's harder still not to wonder how it would all look today if it had just been preserved. Or loved more. Or simply left alone.

And as for what readers will actually find within these pages, that's simple: a list of gone-but-not-forgotten locales around Cincinnati, with as many visual references as available, according to one lifelong citizen who is deeply invested in the city's collective narrative. The stories fall within categories of community and culture: architecture, enterprise, industry, and entertainment. But they are really stories about people and the things they built and enjoyed. They are stories about how Cincinnati grew, is growing,

and will still grow. Most mentions are within living memory, but some are from the city's distant past whose omission would be conspicuous. This list is very far from comprehensive, and will unfortunately never be complete, as time and progress march steadily on. Finally, it's important to remember that destinations that have survived are not untouchable: We must work to treasure Union Terminal and other places like it.

My hope is that local readers turn the last page with a sense of satisfaction that theirs is a city with a long, textured history and above all, a city with far too many stories to be told in any single book.

{FOOD and DRINK}

Courtesy of the Collection of Cincinnati &
Hamilton County Public Library

{FOOD and DRINK}

Where is Cincinnati, anyway? We are neither North nor South (though at one point in our nation's history, that line was clear enough). We're not properly Midwestern either, as we have no Great Plains or Great Lakes. The nearest ocean is many hundreds of miles away. All this could be why it's tricky to nail down our dining culture: Foodways are often an extension of their natural surroundings, and so we're just not known for any particular style or tradition. Our most prominent export is Cincinnati chili, which is highly misunderstood by the rest of the world (their loss).

But what might seem like a liability is actually our superpower: We've always had a little bit of everything, and we've always done it very well. Many of the restaurants that have come and gone—department store tea houses, high-volume cafeterias—represent a way of life that very nearly evolved itself out of existence throughout the 20th century as people embraced car culture and rejected the densely populated city center. As more locals move downtown and walkable urban life roars back in Cincinnati, we remember why we once filled our streets and shops with what feels like countless dining options: European eateries opened by our community of immigrants, beloved neighborhood chili parlors, Jewish delis that migrated around the city, and one of the country's best restaurants.

The history of our dining scene is also the history of Cincinnati's people—where they lived and worked, how they spent their time, and most of all, what they loved to eat.

RESTAURANTS

Bismarck Cafe

An early 20th century icon, Bismarck Cafe featured huge dining rooms (one for gentlemen, one for ladies), an ornate gentleman's bar, and a shadowy rathskeller with a carved arched ceiling (also for the gents). Bismarck was a must-stop destination for downtown diners frequenting the many theaters and opera houses of the time. The site, at the street-level of Walnut Street's Mercantile Building, later became the Colony restaurant.

Caproni's

Caproni's was one of a generation of Italian-American restaurants that bridged the centuries in Cincinnati. Opened in 1886 by Enrico "Cap" Caproni, the eatery moved around to various downtown locations before landing at 610 Main Street. Caproni's continued after World War II under new ownership: Carmella and Antonio Palazzolo made a name for themselves with their locally famous osso bucco. The Palazzolo family retained ownership until 1965, and Caproni's itself remained open until 1975.

Images courtesy of the Collection of Cincinnati & Hamilton County Public Library

Barresi's

Barresi's had a loyal following for its family-style (albeit high-end) Italian-American dining. Odessa and Sal Barresi opened the restaurant in 1963 on Webster Avenue in Deer Park. For 55 years its smallish light green building near the railroad tracks was nearly hidden in plain sight in that unassuming borough. For decades, diners came for the big bowls of penne primavera or linguine with clam sauce, and stayed for the homey ambiance (and sugar-dusted zeppoles). Chef/owner Sarah Wagner, who bought Barresi's in 2005, shut its doors for good in early 2018.

Courtesy of the Collection of Cincinnati & Hamilton County Public Library

Sixty Second Shops

Cincinnati is (in)famous for its take on chili, but a lesser-known local specialty is how we dress our hamburgers: with tartar sauce. The Sixty Second Shops were a chain of 24-hour burger stands conveniently located near neighborhood streetcar stops. The main event was the "Big Sixty," a double-decker hamburger with tartar sauce and shredded iceberg lettuce billed as "A Banquet on a Bun" (think of it as a late-night Frisch's Big Boy). The hamburger format is tried and tested and the business model—located everywhere and always open—needs a serious comeback.

Wong Yie's

Famous Restaurant

Cincinnati was about 50 years late to the Chinese-American food party, but when it arrived in the form of storefront "chop suey" houses in the city's southernmost blocks, it found an intrigued audience. In 1900, Cantonese immigrant Wong Yie helped to create a larger market for Chinese food in the city. Starting with Vine Street's Golden Dragon, which he owned until 1914, and then eventually with the glitzy Wong Yie's Famous Restaurant, Yie and his family ran his array of downtown restaurants until the 1960s.

Myra's Dionysus

For 37 years, Myra's Dionysus held steady on Calhoun Avenue, a fixture for University of Cincinnati students and staff and for Clifton Heights residents alike. Opened in 1977 by Myra Griffin, Myra's was known for vegetarian-friendly Greek-inspired recipes (soups such as curried peanut, avgolemono, and Thai pumpkin were customer favorites), and for a folky-casual atmosphere. It was a healthy option in a sea of fries and pizza slices. Griffin ran the restaurant well into her 80s, until she finally made the move to retire in 2014, closing Myra's for good.

Courtesy of Pixabay

Stenger's Café

For 65 years, Stenger's was a reliable stopover for Over-the-Rhine residents and visitors alike. The saloon, which opened in 1934 and expanded to serve German food starting in 1947, was a neighborhood gathering place, famous as much for its homemade mock turtle soup as its tall glasses of beer. It changed hands a few times in its life (with an attempted reboot in 1999) before abruptly closing after the 2001 riots.

Courtesy of Pixabay

Habig's

For most of the 20th century, Harrison Avenue was a little corner of Germany in Cincinnati. Henry and Sophie Habig opened their eponymous restaurant in 1933, serving up a menu of traditional German dishes like sauerbraten, grilled knockwurst, and mock turtle soup. Owned and operated by three generations of the Habig family, the Westwood restaurant was known around the city for Sophie's Concord grape pie. And right next door was Window Garden, a friendly competitor also offering classic German cuisine that opened up in 1937. Both shops closed up in the early 2000s, taking with them the taste of the Vaterland.

Courtesy of the Collection of Cincinnati & Hamilton County Public Library

Window Garden

Next door to Habig's in Westwood was Window Garden, a traditional take on German dining. Opened in 1937, Window Garden upped the ante on its Euro-style menu, also offering American classics like filet-o-fish (invented by local McDonald's franchisee Lou Groen) and roast turkey. Window Garden also had a Tea Room, and eventually a more contemporary menu that strayed even further from the German classics (though you could always get a dish of red cabbage). The restaurant closed in 2000, just four years before Habig's own departure.

Habits Café

After 40 years as a central business on Oakley Square, Habits abruptly closed up shop in 2019 when the building changed ownership (as of 2022, the space is occupied by the Oakley Fish House). Habits was known for the tried-and-true combo of burgers and beer, plus their "potato rags," a crispy and very messy hash of potatoes, bacon, tomato, onions, and three kinds of melted cheese. Owner Mark Rogers has promised a relocation—and an expanded breakfast menu—in the former Oakley Laundromat across the street.

Images courtesy of Pixabay

The Windjammer

It was an actual ship—or most of one, anyway—parked rather improbably next to the Howard Johnson's in Sharonville. The Windjammer was modeled after an 18th-century Spanish galleon called the El Enfante. Opened in 1966, the restaurant was decked out in nautical artifacts (including some salvaged from the Enfante herself), such as cannons and a 20-foot-tall anchor. The Windjammer was fitted with its own huge dining room and menu of imported seafood. Around thirty years later, after a generation of *very* unique dining, the Windjammer closed in 1997. The "ship" was demolished in 2002.

Rusty's Ristorante

Rusty's was retro, but not on purpose. Rusty Harris opened Rusty's Ristorante on Deer Park's Blue Ash Road in 1984. Former waitress Marlene Smith bought the place and took over in 1997. Regulars showed up nightly for her friendly hospitality and comforting menu of fried chicken, lasagna, and liver and onions—or else parked at the bar for an Old Fashioned or Manhattan. Smith retired in 2014, closing Rusty's after 30 years in business.

Images courtesy of Pixabay

The Rookwood

It was worth a visit just to see the kiln. Set in the original home of Rookwood Pottery (now operating from a new Over-the-Rhine facility), the Rookwood restaurant was an ode to Cincinnati's most famous art export and a chance for diners to see inside the Tudor-style building in Mt. Adams—and even to eat inside one of its massive former kilns. The food was good, too: Chef Jackson Rouse's menu was clever and confident, with favorites like Da Donut French toast, a french toast-style donut with pork belly and bourbon maple syrup. Due to a lease dispute, Rookwood closed in 2016.

Courtesy of Wikimedia, Greg Hume

Campanello's
Italian Restaurant

Known for its "Three Blocks from the Beach" sign, Campanello's was a fixture of downtown dining, serving Italian-American classics since its 1906 opening at 414 Central Avenue. Operated by three generations of the Campanello family, the owners did right by their culinary heritage, making bread, sausage, and pasta right on-site. The interior completed the picture, with wood paneling on the walls and red checkered cloths on the tables. Its small, corner row house-style building offered a glimpse of the *old* old Cincinnati riverfront, before highways and stadiums crowded the landing. After 113 years in business, Campanello's closed in 2019.

Courtesy of Pixabay

Grand Finale

It was a Glendale landmark, a tidy blue building parked right at the corner of Sharon Road. Established in 1975, this "Creperie and Steakery" featured a menu of retro favorites like rack of lamb, a "grand spaghetti toss" (a veggie-friendly mix of artichokes, onions, olives, spinach, and herbs), and of course a menu of a half-dozen crepe options from "Crêpes Coq Au Vin" to "Ham Crêpes Dijon." But the party ended on New Year's Eve 2021, when Grand Finale announced its closure.

Courtesy of Pixabay

Celestial

Like more than a few local restaurants, the Celestial's end came down to a landlord dispute (in this case, an abrupt nonrenewal by owner Chanaka De Lanerolle in 2018). But for most of its 55-year run atop Mt. Adams, the Celestial was known for its high-end menu of steaks and seafood (the "Celestial Oscar" was a filet over king crab with béarnaise sauce) and gorgeous views of downtown's eastern face.

Courtesy of the Collection of Cincinnati & Hamilton County Public Library

Sky Galley

Opened in the early 1940s at the storied Lunken Airport, Sky Galley was housed in the terminal building and had large windows facing the airfield, which allowed diners a clear view of takeoffs and landings. Though popular with patrons young and old, Sky Galley was plagued with operational issues, including an outdated space and the impact of the Covid-19 pandemic. In 2020, despite an online petition from supporters and a funding deal with the city, Sky Galley owner Kirby Brakvill announced that he could no longer keep the restaurant going and closed its doors in September 2020.

Courtesy of the Collection of Cincinnati & Hamilton County Public Library

Central Oyster House

Oysters were once considered cheap eats, and Cincinnati had piles of them thanks to a stagecoach line running directly from the Atlantic coast. Central Oyster House's owner Jake Rosenfeld opened his East Fourth Street restaurant in 1893, and the menu was a geography lesson of seafood locales: Blue Point Oysters, served fresh-shucked, stewed, or fried, plus Cape Charles clams, Kennebec salmon, and Gulf shrimp. Central Oyster House stayed in business—and in the family—all the way up until its closure in 1974.

Courtesy of Pixabay

Parkmoor

Parkmoor was famous for fried chicken, but you could get any fried thing your heart desired, from shrimp to onion rings, plus hamburgers, grilled steaks, and an impressive menu of desserts like Hot Fudge Ice Cream Cake, all manner of pies, something called a "monster malt," and chocolate, strawberry, or pineapple sundaes. The restaurant offered a dining room but was best known for its carryout counter, urging guests to "eat in your car"—a lost art.

Peri's Pancakes

Peri's went above and beyond the typical pancake house repertoire, offering twenty takes on the classic breakfast platter, from "Pigs in Blankets" to "Mexican Fiesta" (cornmeal pancakes with shredded cheese) to Georgia Buckwheat Cakes. You could also get eggs, sandwiches, salads, and even ice cream. Opened in the early 1960s downtown at the corner of Fifth and Main Streets near Government Square, Peri's later moved to the Skywalk between Race and Elm, finally closing up shop in the late 1970s.

Images courtesy of Pixabay

Shuller's Wigwam

Shuller's Wigwam was founded in 1922 as a humble hamburger stand by Max and Anna Shuller. It later expanded to include the memorable teepee-shaped building in College Hill (the teepee was demolished in 1954 to make way for a new building, but the "Wigwam" name remained). Since that reopening, Shuller's Wigwam was known as the place to hold a party, and regular diners remember the complementary relish tray, which offered pickled herring, sauerkraut, and chopped liver, plus a large menu of steaks and seafood. Shuller's passed the restaurant on to sons Leo and Saul and remained open until 2000.

Paula's Café

Stopping in at Paula's on a weekday for a famous "7-minute" burger, made-from-scratch turkey chili, or a quiche-of-the-day at the bar was about as civilized as a quick downtown lunch could get. Sure, you could sit at one of the two-top tables if you had a date, but the bar was about good food with solo-diner expediency. Paula Kirk originally opened the café at Fifth and Vine streets in 1990 and eventually moved (after a brief stop-off at Findlay Market) to east Fourth Street, where she stayed until she closed the restaurant in 2015.

Images courtesy of Pixabay

The Colony

The Colony was about abundance. With five dining rooms (the Victorian Room, Blossom Room, and Washington Room, plus two bars), the restaurant was always open (daily until 1 a.m.) with a huge menu, serving everything from curried lamb to fried chicken. Operating downtown during the 1940s at 420 Walnut Street (in the street-level of the Mercantile Building in the former Bismarck Cafe) and later in the Swifton Center (at Reading and Seymour), the Colony was ideal for large parties looking for a good time.

Courtesy of the Collection of Cincinnati & Hamilton County Public Library

The GOURMET RESTAURANT

The Gourmet Restaurant opened in 1948 on the 20th floor of the Terrace Plaza Hotel, instantly joining Cincinnati's collection of elite downtown restaurants. Known for its wall of circular windows overlooking the city, Gourmet was the picture of elegance, with white tablecloths, black-and-gold dishware, seating for fewer than 50 guests, and a menu of beautiful French food. And then there was the colorful Joan Miró mural, his first US commission, encircling part of the restaurant's interior. The hotel—and the restaurant with it—was closed by the 1990s. The Miró was, blessedly, removed to the Cincinnati Art Museum, but the restaurant and hotel sit empty.

Courtesy of Digital Commonwealth

Wah Mee's

The most consistent thing about Wah Mee's was its fluctuating downtown address. Opened in 1978 on the corner of Fifth and Vine at Fountain Square, Wah Mee's moved one block west to make way for Macy's, then *another* block west to allow Nordstrom room to grow into downtown (which never actually happened). For the next ten years, Wah Mee's held down the block at 435 Elm Street in the "Convention Place" building, and was popular with 9-5-ers and convention-goers alike. However, the building eventually became emblematic of downtown blight and is now slated for demolition and redevelopment. Wah Mee's closed in 2008.

AUTHENTIC
CHINESE FOODS
Open Daily 11 AM to 9:30 PM
Sat. to 11 PM-Sun. to 9:30 PM
WAH MEE
RESTAURANT
Air Conditioned
961-9444
1031 E. McMillan

Trolley Tavern

The Trolley Tavern (formerly Captain Al's) was an Anderson Ferry Road favorite. It was built in 1937 at the intersection of River Road into two wood-paneled trolley cars after the original building was washed away in that year's monumental flood. Over the next few decades, Trolley Tavern expanded to include seating for more than 700 over multiple rooms (the ballroom hosted countless local wedding receptions). Trolley Tavern was known for fresh and fried seafood, ribs, and steaks served in a casual atmosphere.

Images courtesy of the Collection of Cincinnati & Hamilton County Public Library

Doris and Sonny's Home Style Restaurant

The food at Doris & Sonny's unassuming roadside diner was remarkably good. The burgers, fries, omelets, and pies were all handmade from fresh ingredients in the tiny Miamitown eatery. Doris and Sonny Hugentobler opened their restaurant in 1963, serving truckers and motorists until their son Kent took over in 1998. With new management in place, Doris and Sonny's carried on. Kent made his own goetta and tartar sauce; he was frequently seen sitting at the kitchen door peeling a bucket of potatoes or picking a tomato from the back garden. Kent finally closed up shop in 2019, but sold the restaurant to Miamitown-area native Janie Minella. Here's hoping for a reboot.

Le's Pho

What started as a takeaway counter inside the Downtown Main Library building evolved into a brick-and-mortar shop, which turned out steaming bowls of pho soup and toasty banh mi sandwiches. Set in a teeny East Court storefront with a half-dozen tables and a four-seater bar overlooking the street, Le's Pho was standing room only most weekday lunch hours, packed to the gills with keen downtowners. After decades on the job, owners Hai Bui and Le Ha (with help from daughter Huyen Bui-Gauck) finally closed up shop in 2020.

Images courtesy of Pixabay

Isadore's

Joe Isadore began his life's work when he was just 17 years old. In 1959, the day after his high school graduation, Isadore bought a Camp Washington pizzeria from his grandfather and aunt. Then named Pasquale's, the restaurant was one of 27 locations in the area (there's still one in Newport, Kentucky). After a devastating fire in 1978, Joe renamed the new shop Isadore's, and operated the neighborhood landmark for almost 60 years before closing in 2018.

Courtesy of Pixabay

La Petite Pierre

Courtesy of Suzy de Young

This French bistro on Madeira's Camargo Road offered locally sourced, continental classics like mussels Provençal, crispy-skin duck breast, and heirloom tomato consommé—and presented a skillfully designed wine list to go with them. Co-owners (and sisters) Suzy DeYoung and Michele Vollman opened La Petite Pierre in 1988, naming it in honor of their late father, Chef Pierre Adrian, who oversaw Maisonette's first Mobil Travel Guide Five-Star rating in the 1960s. DeYoung departed in 2014 and founded La Soupe, whose mission is to rescue perishable food from groceries and farms that would otherwise go to waste, transforming those ingredients into chef-prepared food to feed the hungry in Cincinnati. After nearly 30 years of success, La Petite Pierre closed its doors in 2018.

The Wheel Café

Through war, prohibition, depression, and more war, the Wheel Café remained. Opened on Walnut Street in 1901 by Meyer Silverglade and Fisher Bacharach (Silverglade's son-in-law), the Wheel started as a saloon to distribute beer from Crown Brewery (one of Silverglade's ventures) and expanded to include a large menu of American fare. The Wheel was the first local establishment to take delivery of a beer shipment after Prohibition was repealed, and the restaurant saw decades of success until it finally closed in 1981.

The Busy Bee

University of Cincinnati students will fondly remember the Busy Bee, a Ludlow Avenue eatery that evolved in its 50 years in Clifton. It started in the 1950s as a straightforward bar and restaurant with live weekend shows, and took on a diner personality in the 1980s. The Busy Bee entertained generations of students and neighborhood residents before it closed in 1998 and was replaced by Thai Café (which departed around 2010).

Courtesy of the Collection of Cincinnati & Hamilton County Public Library

Chester's Road House

The Road House moniker was a bit tongue-in-cheek: Chester's Road House, operated by the Comisar family (à la Maisonette and La Normandie) was an old Montgomery Road farmhouse transformed into a cozy, high-end restaurant, serving up rack of lamb, lobster, and steaks, plus espresso from a gleaming copper machine behind the bar. But the best part was the greenhouse dining room, which had a main floor under filtered natural light and an outer ring of booths tucked into shadowy alcoves. But in 2002, after 30 years in business, Chester's succumbed to growing neighborhood competition and closed. The 140-year-old house was demolished in 2002.

La Petite France

Daniele Crandall opened La Petite France in Evendale on Valentine's Day in 1984. Crandall, who was born in the Pas-de-Calais region of northern France, built the restaurant's acclaimed program of tasting menus, wine dinners, buffets, and events like the annual Bastille Day celebration. After more than 34 years in business, La Petite France closed in 2018.

Images courtesy of Pixabay

JEAN-ROBERT'S RESTAURANT ROSTER

One of Cincinnati's OG celebrity chefs, Jean-Robert de Cavel got his start as The Maisonette's Chef de Cuisine in 1993. After his 2002 exit, the French chef opened an array of beautiful restaurants in Cincinnati, usually more than one at a time and always excellent. Over the next 20 years, many of de Cavel's restaurant concepts came and went, including Lavomatic Café, Pho Paris, Greenup Café, Twist, JeanRo Bistro, Table, and Restaurant L. They were all in downtown or Covington, where they served up everything from steak frites to Vietnamese crêpes. French Crust Café (at Findlay Market) and Le Bar A Boeuf (in Eden Park) remain to carry the de Cavel banner.

La Normandie

La Normandie was the downstairs chophouse counterpart to Maisonette's first-floor French restaurant. The subterranean tavern-style eatery was known for a menu of prime steaks, broiled lobster tail, and classic cocktails. La Normandie was, like Maisonette, also owned and operated by the Comisar family. And like its sister restaurant, it, too, closed in 2005. You can still experience the restaurant's ambiance if you visit acclaimed Italian restaurant Sotto downstairs.

Images courtesy of Pixabay

Maisonette

Nat Comisar founded Maisonette in downtown Cincinnati in 1949 and it remains the final word in the city's 20th century fine dining history. The restaurant earned its first Mobil Travel Guide Five-Star ranking in 1964, going on to embody nouvelle cuisine in Cincinnati and beyond. Though shuttered in 2005, Maisonette still holds the record for most commended restaurant in the nation: With 41 consecutive Five-Star rankings over its 56 years, it was, as Mobil described it, "one of the few flawless dining experiences in the country." Maisonette launched local superstar chefs like Jean-Robert de Cavel and David Falk; its Sixth Street address remains a fine dining destination with Chef Falk's Boca Restaurant.

Pigall's

When Jean-Robert de Cavel re-opened Pigall's in 2002 on downtown's Fourth Street, the restaurant's name had already banked decades of local history. Jean-Robert's version featured two private dining rooms, a coveted Chef's Table with seating for six, and an ambitious menu of French cuisine, featuring local and regional fare, including duck, quail, black cod, and caviar (from a paddlefish farm in Kentucky). But the 2008 recession loomed large, hastening Pigall's to its end—but not before the restaurant earned four Mobil Travel Guide Five-Star ratings and recognition from around the world.

Courtesy of Pixabay

CHILI PARLORS

Courtesy of Pixabay

Make no mistake: Cincinnati chili, as an institution, is alive and well. Not only is Skyline Chili, founded in 1949, the breakout star (chain locations have long since jumped state lines, landing as far as Florida), but independent chili parlors stay rooted in their respective neighborhoods, nursing (mostly) friendly decades-long rivalries.

But the number of chili parlors that have come and gone since Empress Chili's 1922 opening is almost too many to count. Most have been connected in some way to the handful of founding families that, through a tangled history of marriages, inheritances, spinoffs, and buyouts, built a rich culinary and cultural tradition in Cincinnati.

Park Chili

Founded in 1937 by Norman Phillip Bazoff and run by his son Phillip until its sale in 2016, Park Chili was a Northside landmark set in a flatiron building on Hamilton Avenue. For many Park Chili devotees, it was the cooking method that won them over: The Bazoffs browned their beef instead of boiling it (the more common approach). But like most good parlors, Park Chili also offered other foods—namely breakfast. The "Mess" was a memorable hash of eggs, vegetables, meat, and home fries (Phillip claims that this idea was born at Park Chili, along with the concept of chili cheese fries). New owners Steven and Susan Thompson promise a restaurant reboot to come.

EMPRESS CHILI

Skyline may have hit the big-time, but Cincinnati's O.G. chili parlor, from which nearly all subsequent parlors have sprung, was Empress Chili. Opened downtown in 1922 by Macedonian-born brothers Tom and John Kiradjieff, the parlor was well-situated in the 800 block of Vine Street inside the Empress Burlesk Pictures building. The brothers reimagined the already-famous Coney Island hot dog with their Greek-style chili on top, and a local delicacy was born. (They also created chili spaghetti; incidentally, everything was cheeseless.)

Courtesy of Wikimedia, Dann Woellert

A ready-made flow of enthusiastic clientele gave Empress the momentum it needed, and the shop eventually relocated to a new Fifth Street address (now occupied by the Columbia Plaza). Kiradjieff's sons John, Joe, and Eddie carried and expanded the parlor's legacy well into the 20th century. Though most locations have closed, you can still eat Empress Chili today—you just have to go to Alexandria, Kentucky, to get it.

Cretan's

For 71 years, Cretan's Grill occupied a Vine Street corner in Carthage—and pride of place in that neighorhood's history. First opened in 1948 as Cretan's Confectionery by brother and sister John George Cretan and Katina Kyrios, the eatery eventually evolved into a chili parlor, known for their spicy chili and triple-decker sandwiches. Brother-and-sister owners George and Lily Kyrios spent their childhoods at the restaurant, taking over in 1965. Cretan's finally closed in 2019.

Courtesy of Pixabay

The Chili Company

Opened by Pete Poulos and eventually growing to a 12-location chain, The Chili Company (not to be confused with a similarly named Orlando, Florida, eatery) was a neighborhood fixture with a real-deal West Side pedigree: The restaurant was managed in the 1980s by Pete Rose's brother, Dave Rose. The Chili Company was known for its late-night hours catering to a last-call crowd, a menu of all-you-can-eat three-, four-, and five-ways (yep, those dishes had free refills), and the spicy "Torpedo" chili. It closed in the 1990s, and the White Oak building is now Grace of India restaurant, topped by that same prominent vertical sign rising over the intersection of Blue Rock and Cheviot Roads.

Courtesy of Shutterstock

OTHER PARLORS

Liberty Chili Parlor
12 Madison Avenue, Covington

Glenway Chili
4010 Glenway Avenue
Opened 1953 by S. Evon Vulcheff
(became Hilltop Chili in 1958)

Oakley Chili Parlor
3123 Madison Avenue
Opened 1936 (Park Chili in 1937)

Shorty's Chili Kitchen
3158 Madison Road
Owned by Frank B. Knefel; later became The Chili Company (owned by Pete Poulos)

Latonia Chili
3620 Decoursey Avenue, near Kentucky and Latonia Theatre
Opened around 1940 by Samuel Gerros (which beget Price Hill Chili when Gerros's nephew Lazoros Nourtsis opened his own spin-off in 1964)

ABC Chili Parlor
405 Scott Street, Covington
Opened by Alex Chaldekas

Sun Bright Chili
Locations in Madeira, Milford, Fairfield

The Chili Bowl
6110 Vine Street, Elmwood Place
Opened 1938

Orpheum Chili
905 East McMillan Avenue, across the street from the Paramount Building
Opened in early 1940s

Gayety Chili
Former Empress space in the 1940s
Operated by Demetrios L. Vaias into the 1950s; closed in 1960s and replaced with Sunset Chili

20th Century Chili Shop
1940s
Inside 20th Century Theater building in Oakley
Operated by Catherine and John Pashal

BAKERIES AND CANDY

It's easy to assume that today's bakery kingpins—Busken and Servatii—stand alone. But the truth is much sweeter: There are a host of smaller pastry shops, some established like the BonBonerie and Holtman's Donuts and some rising stars like Brown Bear Bakery and Blue Oven Bakery, that keep the city in cakes, cookies, bread, and doughnuts all year round. These shops, large and small, follow in the footsteps of long-lost bakeries and candy stores—and some literally follow the old recipes that these kitchens made famous in Cincinnati.

Virginia Bakery

For nearly 80 years, Clifton's Virginia Bakery was the final word in schnecken in Cincinnati. Somehow both cake and pastry, the treat is an extra-buttery take on the classic cinnamon roll. ("*Schnecke*" is the German word for "snail.") Virginia Bakery, operated by the Thie family, specialized in old German pastries, and their iconic white box with red lettering was a happy sight for generations of Cincinnatians. Though Virginia Bakery closed in 2005, you can still find schnecken at Busken Bakery, which acquired the recipe and revives the treat each holiday season.

Images courtesy of Pixabay

Mehas Brothers Confectionery

In 1886, a trio of Greek brothers—Peter, George, and Nicholas Mehas—started a candy shop on Fountain Square known for its array of handmade candies, chocolates, and ice creams. They quickly expanded. In the early 1900s, the Mehas brothers had stores throughout downtown on Fifth Street (next to the Bijou Theater), on Vine Street, and as far afield as Hamilton, Ohio. The Mehas brothers eventually entwined with another candy family dynasty: the Aglamesis brothers. Thomas Aglamesis married Viola Mehas, and their son Jim went on to own Oakley's Aglamesis Bro's Ice Cream and Candy.

Little Dutch Bakery

Located in a small storefront location on Hamilton Avenue in Mt. Healthy, Little Dutch Bakery was a neighborhood fixture known for colorful cakes, pastries, breads, and cookies. (The Beehive Coffee Cake, one of more than a dozen daily coffee cake varieties, was a fan favorite.) Owner Chris Girmann was the third generation of his family to operate Little Dutch since its opening in 1910. But after more than 100 years in business, the bakery was forced to close during the Covid-19 pandemic.

Images courtesy of Amy Brownlee

Klosterman's Dixie Bakery and Coffee Shop

The Dixie Terminal Building—a barrel-vaulted beauty still standing on Fourth Street—once played host to a retail arm of the Klosterman Baking Company: Klosterman's Dixie Bakery and Coffee Shop. It offered breakfast and lunch and an array of baked goods, and for some years even an afternoon tea service. From the late 1920s until the 1970s, when the Terminal housed the Cincinnati Stock Exchange, railroad ticket agencies, and administrative offices of the Cincinnati Street Railway Company, the Dixie Bakery was a civilized little corner of downtown.

Mullane's

Known for their nectar sodas (flavored with vanilla and bitter almond, and tasting of pound cake), Mullane's also kept the city stocked with high-quality candy. Opened in 1848 by William and Mary Fitzpatrick Mullane, the West End shop eventually moved to Fourth Street in the 1890s. Mullane's sold bonbons, taffy, "nectar drops" (hard candies), and "Woodland Goodies" (nut brittle candies). Family infighting started the company's breakup in 1935. After 50 years of ownership changes and an eventual bankruptcy, Mullane's was fully dissolved by 1983.

Images courtesy of Pixabay

Shadeau Bakery

You had to get up pretty early in the morning to get a Shadeau baguette. Opened in 1993 in a narrow Over-the-Rhine storefront, Shadeau Breads quickly earned a reputation for fresh bread made with quality ingredients. The Main Street shop, started by former Virginia Bakery staffer Bill Pritz, usually sold out of its French bread, sourdough, brioche, pizza dough, focaccia, and pastries well before lunchtime. Pritz retired in 2017, selling Shadeau to his longtime accountant Brett Arnow, who initially looked to keep the bakery going with wife, Elisa. Nevertheless, Shadeau closed in 2018.

DELIS AND CAFETERIAS

Cafeterias get a bad rap. But for a quick, unfussy lunch, they can't be beat, thanks to convenience, speed, and (usually) tasty menus. A cousin to the cafeteria, the deli, is one legacy of Cincinnati's Jewish community, which has largely moved out of downtown and Avondale and into northern neighborhoods like Amberley Village and Sycamore Township. Downtown was once peppered with delis, such as the beloved Bilker's or Temple Deli, serving traditional Jewish foods to workers and residents alike.

Mills Cafeteria

Marysville, Ohio, native James O. Mills spied an untapped market in Cincinnati, and opened Mills Cafeteria to meet it. In 1915, his Government Square eatery offered high-quality home cooking, priced to sell, in a clean and beautiful setting. The venture was so successful that in 1921, Mills traded up to a much larger building on East Fourth Street, trimmed with Dutch windmill-themed Rookwood tiles and recognizable by the rotating neon windmill sign out front. From the 1940s until its 1967 closure, Mills Cafeteria was a lunchtime oasis for downtown shoppers and workers.

Courtesy of the Collection of Cincinnati & Hamilton County Public Library

Pilder's Cafeteria

Pilder's Cafeteria was opened downtown in 1928 by Charles Pilder, later moving to Avondale after World War II, and eventually to what is now the Dillonvale Shopping Center (near Deer Park High School). Known for its corned beef (pickled on-site) and hot deli sandwiches, Pilder's menu included knishes, brisket, noodle kugel, and other traditional Jewish foods. By the mid-1990s, it was the only kosher butcher/deli/grocery in town. However, just like dozens of peers and competitors, Pilder's closed before the end of that decade.

Bilker's

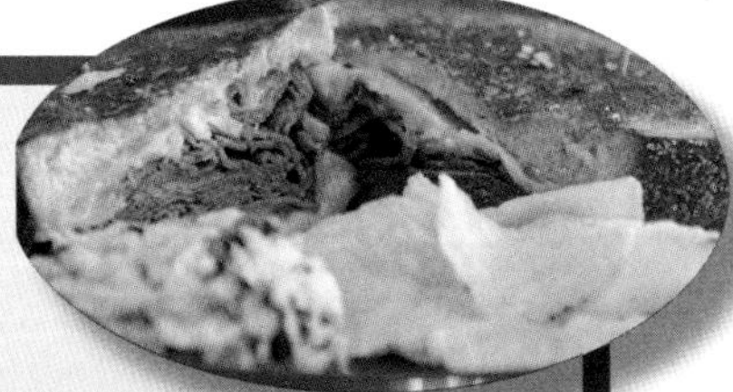

Founded in 1900 by George and Jenny Bilker on downtown's Central Avenue, Bilker's was in the kosher deli business all the way up to 2008 when the third location (in Roselawn) finally closed. The shop was known for its array of Jewish classics like hot corned beef, fish smoked in-house, and a menu of sandwiches, but mostly for its staying power: As other kosher delis came and went throughout the city, Bilker's remained a steady presence, serving Cincinnati's Jewish population for more than 100 years.

Images courtesy of Pixabay

Temple Delicatessen and Sandwich Shop

Founded in the 1930s, Temple Delicatessen and Sandwich Shop had a prominent and longstanding presence in the downtown lunch-break scene, heralded by a large neon sign hanging from its West Seventh Street walk-up across from the Shillito's Department Store. Visitors perused a cold deli case of meats and cheeses, plus fresh baked breads and a menu of double-deckers (not to mention a huge list of available kosher foods), or sat at the counter or tables and enjoyed homemade soups, potato salad, or freshly made cheese blintzes. Temple closed in 2006.

Loretta's

This North Avondale deli catered to the Jewish community, but Loretta Ebner herself was a Catholic. Nevertheless, her Jewish-style cuisine attracted customers from all over the city to Paddock and Reading Roads, where she ran her deli for 40 years. Opened in 1926, Loretta's was known for triple-decker sandwiches and even a catering service. Loretta was there all along the way. Even after a hip replacement in the 1960s, Loretta helped with catering for another decade. She passed away in 1988.

Courtesy of Pixabay

LOCAL PRODUCTS

Our most (in)famous export is Cincinnati chili, and if you know, you know. But we didn't stop there: From ice cream to potato chips to sparkling wine, Cincinnati's locally made products have always been ready to party.

Catawba Wine-Longworth Vineyards

Early Cincinnati settler Nicholas Longworth thought his hillside Mt. Adams property an ideal spot for wine cultivation. He planted his first vineyards there in 1813, adding Catawba vines in 1825. His peers agreed, drinking up Longworth's sparkling Catawba from as far away as California and even Europe. Poet Henry Wadsworth Longfellow even penned "Ode to Catawba Wine." But crop blights and failures, the Civil War, and Longworth's own death meant the end of Cincinnati's Catawba wine. That is, until local winemaker Kate MacDonald launched Skeleton Root in 2016, where she grows and ages her own "Heritage Catawba."

Courtesy of Pixabay

French-Bauer Dairy

English-born Thomas French started his Cincinnati dairy in 1842, delivering farm-fresh milk to local neighborhoods. French merged with the Bauer Ice Cream and Baking Company around 1900 and throughout most of the 20th century, French-Bauer products were omnipresent at local drug stores and soda fountains. After many generations of family ownership over a whopping 137 years in business, French-Bauer was sold in 1979 to Meyer Dairy.

Husman's Potato Chips

They weren't fancy, but that was hardly the point. In 1919, Harry Husman started the Husman Potato Products Company when he was just 24 years old and proceeded to build a local potato chip empire. Young Harry had big ideas where potatoes were concerned, and started out using a rope and pulley system to haul the heavy bags up to his kitchen. The young entrepreneur scaled up quickly, installing automatic frying and packaging machines that helped make Husman's a household name in Cincinnati. After a few ownership changes, Pennsylvania-based Utz took over Husman's from Conagra Brands in 2019. In 2021, Utz discontinued the 102-year-old Husman's brand.

Images courtesy of Pixabay

MARKETS

Before major grocery stores started selling everything under one roof, markets were the way that many Cincinnatians used to buy their fresh food (and non-perishables were sold at dry goods retailers). As with other amenities like movie theaters and bakeries, markets dotted each neighborhood, giving residents easy, regular access to produce, meat, and dairy products from the farms surrounding the city. Downtown alone had five markets on this list, and only Findlay Market, in operation since 1855, remains.

Jabez Elliott Flower Market

Opened in 1894, this market opened thanks to a $10,000 gift from local widow Mary Holroyd in memory of her departed husband, Jabez Elliott. Located along West Sixth Street between Elm and Plum Streets, Jabez Elliott was widely considered to be one of the largest venues of its kind in the country—that is, an indoor market dedicated to selling only flowers. It met its own end in 1950, when it was demolished to make way for a parking lot.

Courtesy of the Collection of Cincinnati & Hamilton County Public Library

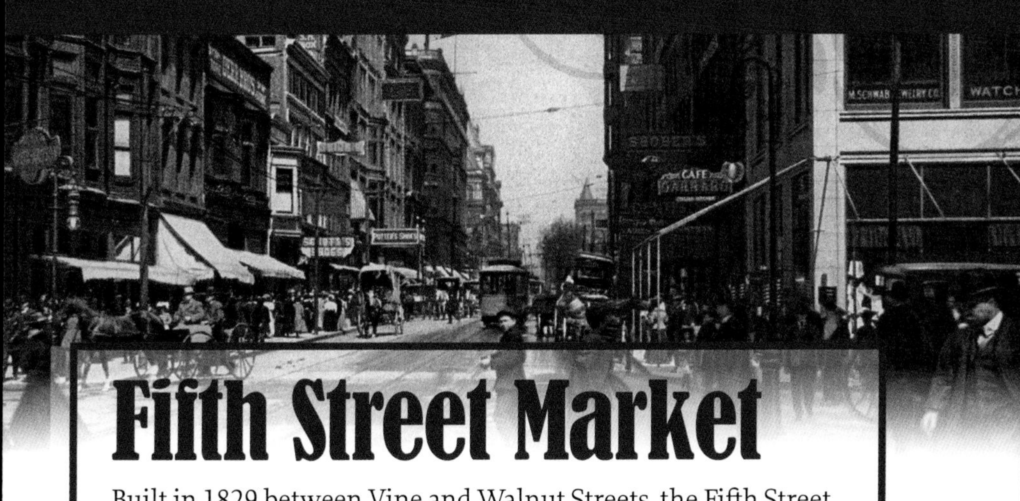

Fifth Street Market

Built in 1829 between Vine and Walnut Streets, the Fifth Street Market was one of Cincinnati's earliest public markets, helping to put the city's pork-packing industry on the map. It was also known locally as "Upper Market," and it served many public roles during the Civil War, notably as a mustering point for Union troops. It was demolished in 1870 to eventually make way for the first incarnation of Fountain Square (when it was a narrow esplanade surrounding the Tyler Davidson Fountain).

Court Street Market

Built in 1864, Court Street Market was located between Vine and Walnut Streets downtown in what is now a corridor of parking meters. According to historians at Findlay Market, stone tunnels were built underneath the structure to run hogs between slaughterhouses. Court Street Market was closed way back in 1912 and demolished two years later, but the street scene is much the same (if you're looking at the south block, that is): A notable former neighbor is Avril-Bleh Meat Market, which has been a going concern downtown since 1894 and gives a small glimpse of Court Street's former glory.

Courtesy of the Collection of Cincinnati & Hamilton County Public Library

Covington Market House

Built in 1861 on Sixth Street in Covington, Kentucky's West End neighborhood, the Covington Market House survived the Civil War. By 1875 it was a booming neighborhood amenity, hosting 16 butchers and dozens of area farmers and other vendors. By the next century, however, the market house building was in disrepair, and the city tore it down in 1907. The site is now home to George Steinford Park (otherwise known as the Sixth Street Promenade), a tree-lined gateway into Covington's MainStrasse Village.

Courtesy of the Collection of Cincinnati & Hamilton County Public Library

Pearl Street Market

Built in stages as early as 1816, Pearl Street Market replaced an earlier, informal public market that was established near the river in 1804. Located in The Bottoms neighborhood on Pearl Street between Broad and Sycamore Streets (today's location would be in Great American Ballpark, somewhere around left field), Pearl Street Market catered to river travelers and area families alike. A few members of Cincinnati royalty got their start in or around the market: Buddy LaRosa started a produce market, the Lindner brothers ran an ice cream shop (a predecessor to UDF), and Bernard Kroger opened his first store. When it was torn down in 1934, Pearl Street Market was the city's oldest public market.

Norwood Market House

The Norwood Market House building still stands at the corner of Mills and Walter Avenues, just east of Montgomery Road in Norwood. It was constructed at the turn of the 20th century and used first as a year-round, indoor market house for vendors of fresh meats, fruits, vegetables, and other produce. Soon after its construction, however, it ceased market operations, and by World War I was everything but, including a church, an ice-skating rink, a roller rink, a storage facility, a vehicle safety inspection center, and an amateur boxing club.

Images courtesy of the Collection of Cincinnati & Hamilton County Public Library

Sixth Street Market

A neighbor to the Jabez Elliott Flower Market and built just a year later in 1895, Sixth Street Market was a large and ornately designed outdoor market with 64 vendor stalls. Also known as "Western Market," Sixth Street Market was possibly Cincinnati's most beautiful market building, but it was also among the many victims of the city's 20th-century highway expansion: The structure was demolished in 1960 to clear a path for Interstate 75.

Courtesy of the Collection of Cincinnati & Hamilton County Public Library

TAVERNS, BARS, AND BEER GARDENS

Much of Cincinnati's tavern culture emerged directly from its breweries: Those beer barons needed customers, and a hometown bar (often with a free lunch thrown in) assured a steady stream of interest and income. A few of these establishments were open long enough to see Cincinnati's great brewing culture form in the late 19th-century as well as witness its rebirth in the 21st century.

WASHINGTON PLATFORM

The Johan Armleder Wine & Lager Beer Saloon opened in the mid-1800s on the south side of the Erie Canal (now Central Parkway), across from Over-the-Rhine. It was one of hundreds of neighborhood saloons at the time as the city's beer-loving German population exploded. In 1875, the saloon changed its name to Washington Platform; much later, it became known for an annual Oyster Festival, which started in 1986. After weathering Prohibition, two World Wars, and a depopulated downtown, Washington Platform finally decided to close its doors in 2021.

Courtesy of Amy Brownlee

Lenhardt's & Christy's

This Clifton Heights building had a layered local history pedigree: It was built in the 1890s by beer baron Christian Moerlein as a gift for his daughter and son-in-law, and later became the much-beloved Lenhardt's & Christy's (specifically Lenhardt's German Hungarian Restaurant and Christy's Rathskeller), serving a menu of European dishes like Hungarian goulash and spaetzle. The restaurant closed in 2013 and its assets were sold at auction. But the building was expensive to maintain, and after much struggle between preservationists and the owners, who wished to sell the property for development, it was demolished in 2014.

Grammer's

Grammer's was opened in 1872 by Anton Grammer, and was perfectly poised to ride Cincinnati's beer-brewing wave. The barroom and billiard hall were popular haunts, and the elaborate stained-glass windows facing Walnut Avenue were a local point of interest. In the 1950s, then owner Charles Berkman expanded Grammer's to serve a menu of traditional German foods. The bar changed owners—and concepts—multiple times (finally landing with former city councilman Jim Tarbell) until it finally shut down for good in the 2010s.

Images courtesy of the Collection of Cincinnati & Hamilton County Public Library

TEA ROOMS AND COFFEE HOUSES

Downtown was once a true shopping scene, with white-gloved ladies visiting the grand department stores that mostly sat along West Fourth Street (which became the West Fourth Street Historic District in 1976). And one reason why the shopping culture was so elegant was the array of tea rooms available. Shoppers refreshed themselves at places like the Woman's Exchange, McAlpin's, and Mabley & Carew's Fountain Room, glamorous food courts that served everything from chicken salad to mock turtle soup.

McAlpin's Tea Room

Advertising itself as having "Cincinnati's most elegant moderate priced Dining Rooms," McAlpin's large tea room was on the upper floors of the West Fourth Street store (complete with an express elevator straight to the dining room floor between the hours of 11:30 a.m. and 2 p.m.), and featured entertainment like weekly tapings of Bob Braun's *Good Morning Show*, which aired on 700 WLW Radio.

Courtesy of the Collection of Cincinnati & Hamilton County Public Library

Shillito's Tea Room

Located on the sixth floor of the Shillito's downtown department store, Shillito's Tea Room was known for its bold art deco design and feeling of spaciousness created by tall ceilings and large windows. And on some evenings, the room opened for a special candlelight dinner. You could get a meal there as late as the 1990s, when the room was known as the 6th Floor Cafe in Lazarus.

Courtesy of the Collection of Cincinnati & Hamilton County Public Library

The Woman's Exchange

By the mid-20th-century, most of downtown's department stores featured a tea room. But the Woman's Exchange was there first. The shop opened in 1883, later moving to its iconic West Fourth Street location in 1906, becoming instantly recognizable for its large bay window. The model was unique: Both a cafe and a market, the Woman's Exchange gave a place for women to sell their own handmade goods, like embroidered linens. The city's wealthy set came to shop and socialize. The Exchange relocated to Hyde Park in the late 1960s, and finally closed in 1985.

Courtesy of Pixabay

The MABLEY & CAREW FOUNTAIN ROOM

Mabley & Carew featured a soda fountain and lunch counter as early as 1912. But it wasn't until 50 years later that the department store launched its famed Fountain Room tea room and restaurant to coincide with its 1962 relocation from Carew Tower to the completely remodeled Rollman's lot at Fifth and Vine. The new shop had an all-new look, and shoppers were thrilled with the mod style and Fountain Square view.

Kaldi's Coffee House

One shop that was emblematic of Over-the-Rhine's 1990s cultural resurgence was Kaldi's. Before 3CDC overhauled Vine Street, Kaldi's was on Main Street, serving a band of dedicated patrons—dubbed the "Lost Boys" by longtime bartender Brian Knueven. Founded in 1994 by Mike Markiewicz and Sonya McDonnell, Kaldi's was a hub of neighborhood personalities, filled with old books and records and pouring coffee by day and stronger drinks by night. Though it survived the 2001 civil unrest that consumed much of the neighborhood, Kaldi's never fully regained its audience and shuttered in 2008.

Courtesy of Pixabay

{ENTERTAINMENT}

Courtesy of the Collection of Cincinnati & Hamilton County Public Library

{ENTERTAINMENT}

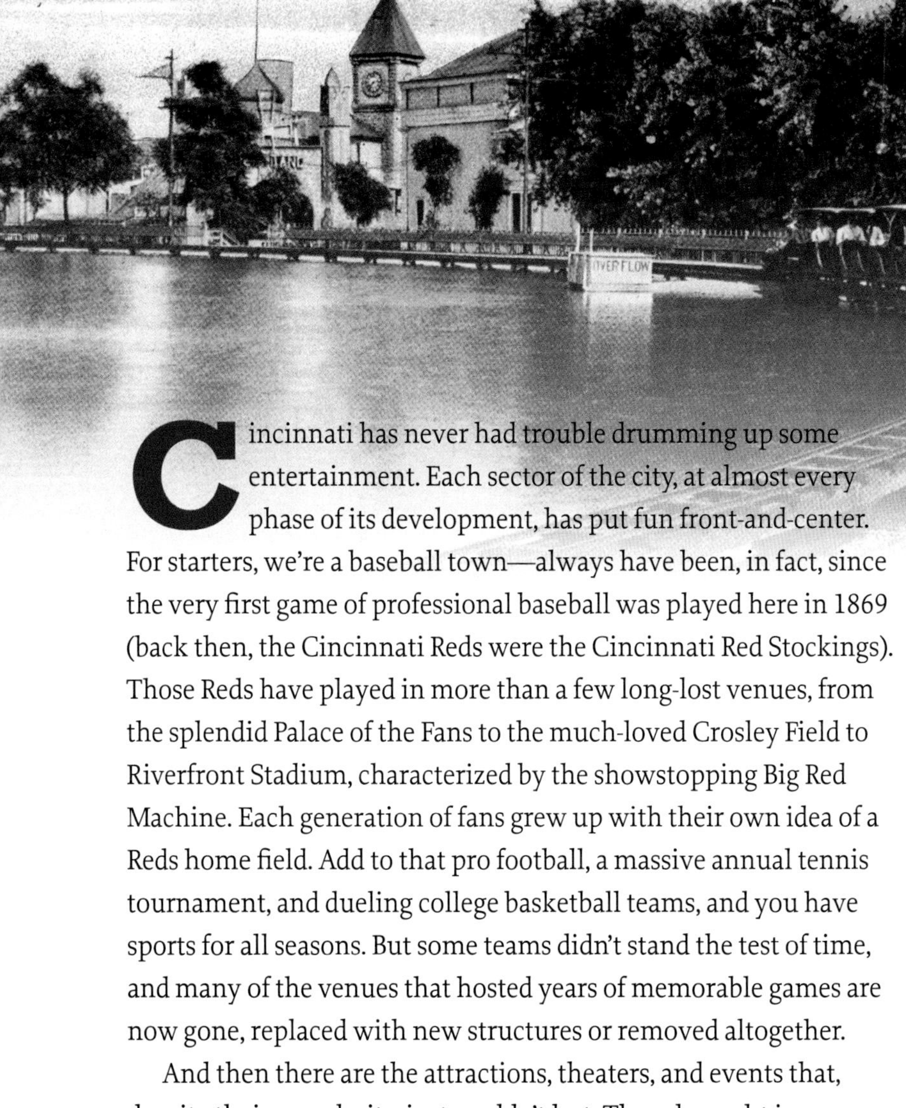

Cincinnati has never had trouble drumming up some entertainment. Each sector of the city, at almost every phase of its development, has put fun front-and-center. For starters, we're a baseball town—always have been, in fact, since the very first game of professional baseball was played here in 1869 (back then, the Cincinnati Reds were the Cincinnati Red Stockings). Those Reds have played in more than a few long-lost venues, from the splendid Palace of the Fans to the much-loved Crosley Field to Riverfront Stadium, characterized by the showstopping Big Red Machine. Each generation of fans grew up with their own idea of a Reds home field. Add to that pro football, a massive annual tennis tournament, and dueling college basketball teams, and you have sports for all seasons. But some teams didn't stand the test of time, and many of the venues that hosted years of memorable games are now gone, replaced with new structures or removed altogether.

And then there are the attractions, theaters, and events that, despite their popularity, just couldn't last. These brought in many thousands of visitors to our city and region and put on a show for all the world to see. Through it all, Cincinnatians have lived exceedingly entertaining lives, making the most of their pretty city by the river.

Courtesy of the Collection of Cincinnati & Hamilton County Public Library

AMUSEMENT PARKS

The reigning amusement park in Cincinnati is of course Kings Island, which opened in Mason in 1972, partly in response to Coney Island's destructive flooding in 1964. Many of the original Coney rides, including the Log Flume, the Carousel, Giant Slide, Flying Scooter, and Dodgem, were relocated to King's Island's midway. The city's amusement park legacy was at once dismantled and preserved (for the time being, at least). Kings Island now sits on the shoulders of those parks that came before it—some humble, some wildly popular, all up for a good time.

Courtesy of the Collection of Cincinnati & Hamilton County Public Library

Ludlow Lagoon

Once one of the country's largest amusement parks, Ludlow Lagoon opened its 85-acre, man-made lake in 1895 with bathing beaches and a boathouse, plus a dance hall, theater, scenic railway, clubhouse, and its own streetcar route. (Ludlow Lagoon was, in fact, opened by the Cincinnati Street Railway Company to spur tourism; at its height, the #3 Ludlow Line picked up passengers every few minutes from downtown's Fountain Square.) It took a 1913 Ohio River flood and a 1915 tornado—not to mention a World War—to bring the end of Ludlow Lagoon in 1918.

CONEY ISLAND RIDES

Coney Island's first roller coaster, Dip the Dips, opened in 1911, followed by the Coney Island Cyclone in 1927. For decades, generations of locals enjoyed rides like the Shooting Star, the Wildcat, and Lost River. The midway evolved over the years (some rides decamping to the then new Kings Island in 1972). The park was best known for Sunlite Pool, a Coney Island institution that kept locals cool since since 1925. However, leadership decided in 2019 to double-down on the more successful water attractions and remove all of its old-fashioned rides once and for all.

Images courtesy of the Collection of Cincinnati & Hamilton County Public Library

Fantasy Farm

For families who were a bit too young for the likes of the Screechin' Eagle (see next door's LeSourdsville Lake/Americana), Fantasy Farm was just the ticket. Specializing in rides and attractions for children ages 12 and under, the Middletown amusement park was a kinder, gentler (not to mention cheaper) day out, with a petting zoo, picnic area, and kid-friendly rides like bumper cars and a carousel. A change in ownership in 1982 set the stage for Fantasy Farm's eventual 1991 closure.

Courtesy of Amy Brownlee

LeSourdsville Lake

Like its downriver counterpart Coney Island, Middletown's LeSourdsville Lake Amusement Park started with small family attractions and expanded to include games and rides. The park opened in 1922 and by the 1940s it sported a ballroom and Ferris wheel, and it continued to thrive well into the 1970s (even with shiny new neighbor Kings Island looming in Mason). After some long periods of disorder, including a name change ("Americana"), a destructive 1990 electrical fire, and a bankruptcy filing, LeSourdsville Lake closed in 2002.

Chester Park

When Coney Island added Sunlite Pool in 1925, Chester Park had been going strong as a local swimming attraction for 30 years. Opened in 1875 at Spring Grove and West Mitchell Avenues as a racing club, Chester Park was acquired in 1895 by the Cincinnati Street Railway Company, which then relaunched it as an amusement park with roller coasters, rides (e.g., the Tickler), and a swimming/boating lake. It even had its own train station (now housed at Heritage Village Museum). Money troubles forced the park's closure in 1932. The Chester Park pool reopened the next year but then closed for good in 1941.

Courtesy of the Collection of Cincinnati & Hamilton County Public Library

ATTRACTIONS

There was opera at the Cincinnati Zoo (who could forget when the sopranos were joined in song by trumpeting elephants and screaming monkeys?). There was Tall Stacks, which filled the Ohio with a fleet of riverboats, taking the city back in time. And there was the Cincinnati Museum of Natural History and Planetarium, an Eden Park institution famously escorted by larger-than-life wooly mammoths. Attractions and entertainment have kept Cincinnati humming since its earliest days, and these bygone events and destinations created memories for generations of locals.

Courtesy of the Collection of Cincinnati & Hamilton County Public Library

Highland House

This is a long lost landmark, but it represents an exciting era of Cincinnati's entertainment scene. One of the city's hilltop "incline resorts," the Highland House sat atop Mt. Adams and commanded a view of the Ohio River and the urban basin below. (It shared the same hill with the original Rookwood Pottery building, which was established in 1880.) Guests turned out for live orchestral music, food and drink, theater, and dancing. Highland House closed in 1895 and was later demolished; the site now holds the Highland Towers apartments.

Bellevue House

Visible for miles, this multi-tiered resort capping the Bellevue Incline stretched from Elm Street up to the current Bellevue Hill Park in Clifton Heights. Opened in 1876, the Bellevue House was designed by James W. McLaughlin (whom we also have to thank for the old Cincinnati Art Academy building) and connected the basin with uptown destinations like the Cincinnati Zoo and the University of Cincinnati. Bellevue House hosted thousands of patrons as they dined, danced, and viewed concerts in the grand hall. In 1901, in what must have been a spectacular sight, it burned to the ground.

Images courtesy of the Collection of Cincinnati & Hamilton County Public Library

TALL STACKS

First held in 1988 as a part of the general merrymaking around Cincinnati's bicentennial, Tall Stacks was a celebration of riverboats past and present (namely the *Belle of Louisville* and the *Delta Queen*). The multi-day festival featured boat races, tours, and cruises; it was held every three or four years until the last event in 2006, when attempts to revive it stalled due to lack of sponsorship. During its heyday in the 1990s, Tall Stacks attracted hundreds of thousands to the city (the 1992 event saw 800,000 attendees), national musical artists like B. B. King and Emmylou Harris, and more than a dozen traveling riverboats.

Courtesy of Wikimedia

Billy Bryant Showboat

If Cincinnati ever had a river king, it was Billy Bryant. *The New York Times* even wrote up a profile of Bryant in 1937, describing him as the "Showboat Master of the Ohio." Captain Billy Bryant operated his floating theater from 1918 until 1942, sailing inland rivers—or rather, being hauled up by an attached steamboat—and stopping along the way to entertain with zany, family-friendly live stage shows. Bryant closed up shop in 1942, and the showboat was pressed into service as a wharf boat in Huntington, West Virginia, where it sank in 1949.

Courtesy of the Collection of Cincinnati & Hamilton County Public Library

INDUSTRIAL EXPOSITIONS

Music Hall was built in 1877 to house the city's fabled choirs and singing societies. But it was also built to host industrial expositions, which had gathered steam in Cincinnati in the 19th century. The Great Centennial Exposition of 1888 was very grand indeed, transforming Music Hall with more than 1,000 exhibits. (The most stunning of which was from the Thomas Edison Company: 150,000 light bulbs that likely introduced more than a few Cincinnatians to electric light) and a fleet of Italian-imported gondolas that ferried guests along the canal.

Courtesy of the Collection of Cincinnati & Hamilton County Public Library

THE CINCINNATI MUSEUM OF NATURAL HISTORY AND PLANETARIUM

The cast of characters was impossible to miss: Elsinore Arch, a stone tower standing sentinel on Gilbert Avenue, flanked by an angular 1957 building and a family of wooly mammoths. The setting was the Museum of Natural History and Planetarium, once home to Cincinnati's collection of all things science, nature, and history (which itself has deep roots; John James Audubon was an early museum staffer). The beloved collection moved to the Cincinnati Museum Center in 1990, and the building and planetarium were eventually replaced with a new WCPO newsroom. And those wooly mammoths? They migrated a few miles west to the front lawn of the Geier Collections & Research Center.

Cincinnati Zoo Bandshell

Courtesy of the Collection of Cincinnati & Hamilton County Public Library

The Cincinnati Zoo's formal botanical gardens were the perfect setting for outdoor concerts in the ornate bandshell, which was large enough to hold an entire orchestra. The building, constructed in 1911 near today's Children's Zoo and Gibbon Island, hosted evening concerts and social gatherings for the zoo's culture vultures. At home among other remarkable structures at the zoo—the 1975 Reptile House (formerly the Monkey House) and 1906 Elephant House (formerly the Herbivora House) come to mind—the bandshell helped make the Cincinnati Zoo one of the nation's loveliest.

MOVIE THEATERS AND DRIVE-INS

Many local stages and screens have amused the Cincinnati masses. Through much of the 20th century, movie theaters were in practically every neighborhood (and some even floating merrily down the Ohio River). You can see remnants of this lifestyle with surviving small-format venues like Esquire Theatre, in Clifton, and Mariemont Theatre. Downtown hosted a theater district that drew spectators from all corners of the city—and at all hours. Our present-day cultural offerings owe much to these forerunners.

Courtesy of the Collection of Cincinnati & Hamilton County Public Library

B. F. Keith's Theater

Keith's Theater started its life in old Cincinnati and ended it at the edge of a new era for the city. Opened in 1892 at the corner of Fifth and Walnut Streets downtown, it was originally named the Fountain Square Theatre. A few ownership changes finally landed it in the hands of Benjamin Franklin Keith, and over the next 40 years, the theater underwent renovations and technology upgrades to keep up with the times (including being outfitted with a Wurlitzer theater organ). Keith's finally closed in 1965 and the building was demolished in 1966 to make way for the new Fountain Square Plaza.

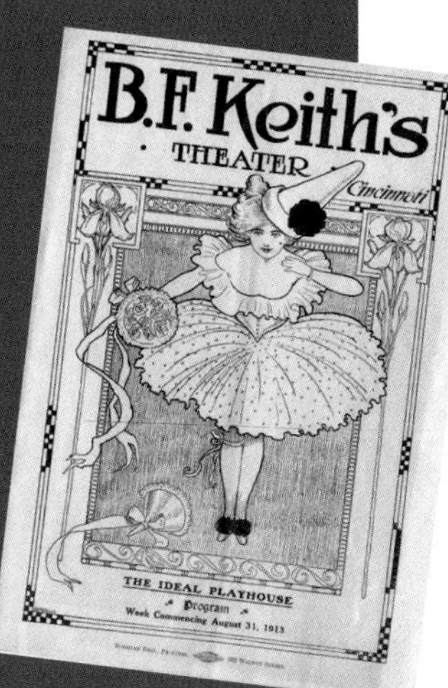

Albee Theater

Most of our movie houses—or movie palaces if you're talking about Fountain Square's almighty Albee Theater—are long gone, traded in for larger, multi-screen outfits. The E. F. Albee Photoplays Theater opened in 1927 on the south side of the Fountain Square esplanade, equipped with a movie screen, vaudeville stage, and orchestra pit with a genuine Wurlitzer organ (now housed in the Music Hall Ballroom). RKO took over in 1930 and booked movies and stage acts until it closed the theater in 1974. Though the building was demolished in 1977 to make way for the Westin Hotel, you can still see the classic marquee installed along the south wall of the Duke Energy Convention Center.

Images courtesy of the Collection of Cincinnati & Hamilton County Public Library

Western Woods Cinema

Opened two days before Christmas in 1966, with breathless anticipation of "acres of free parking, push-back seats, and all-weather comfort!" Western Woods Cinema was a modern family's movie experience: convenient, spacious, and temperature-controlled. The Glenway Avenue cinema showed first-run films and sat more than 1,200 in its single-screen theater. The building was later converted into a Thriftway grocery store and eventually a Home Depot.

Dixie Gardens Drive-in and Ice Bowl

Dixie Gardens opened in 1947 in Fort Wright, Kentucky, billed as "The Auto Show Place of the Middle West." (The opening night feature was *Three Little Girls in Blue*, a Technicolor musical comedy starring Norwood native Vera-Ellen, eight years before her career-making role in *White Christmas.*) With a 750-car capacity, midnight shows every Thursday through Saturday, and the Ice Bowl skating rink right next door, Dixie Gardens was hopping every weekend. It was demolished just after its 40th birthday in 1988.

Shubert Theater

Courtesy of the Collection of Cincinnati & Hamilton County Public Library

Set in the city's original YMCA (which was built in the 1840s), Shubert Theater was located on East Seventh Street downtown, very near where the Aronoff Center for the Arts sits today. Opened in 1921, Shubert added a theater screen in the 1930s; it was operated by Shubert Brothers Theater Company, now called the Shubert Organization, which owns theaters all over the country. Shubert staged films and theater productions well into the 1970s before its closure in 1975. The building was demolished a year later.

Palace Theater

Opened on Sixth Street in 1919 with an ornate interior, the five-story, 2,600-seat Palace Theater was designed for live performances and converted to a movie theater in the late 1920s. In 1978, when the Palace seemed doomed to demolition, the city (including then mayor Gerald "Jerry" Springer) and business owners mobilized to attempt a rescue, reopening the theater under the new name "International Music House." Despite being listed on the National Register of Historic Places, the beloved Palace Theater building did not live to see the 21st century: It was demolished in 1982 and eventually replaced with the Center at 600 Vine office building.

Capitol Theater

Capitol Theater opened at Seventh and Vine downtown in 1921. It later became a Cinerama theater, advertising itself as the only venue for 300 miles with the three-projector technology and a wide, curved screen that gave audiences an immersive viewing experience—"no glasses needed." It was a big deal: The opening night in 1954 boasted "state dignitaries" from Ohio, Kentucky, and Indiana and local news telecasts. The Capitol Cinerama had 14 showings each week, and prices ranged from $1.20 to $2.65. The show went on until 1967, when the theater closed. It was torn down in 1970.

Courtesy of the Collection of Cincinnati & Hamilton County Public Library

Oakley Drive-In

Its main claim-to-fame is that it was the last man standing. When it was finally closed in 2005, Oakley Drive-In was the last remaining drive-in theater within the city. Opened in 1956 (the blog Cinema Treasures reports that the opening film was a double-feature: *The Man Who Knew Too Much* and *The Proud Ones*), it did not have an auspicious beginning. Much of the neighborhood fought against its right to exist (to be fair, a screen the size of a scoreboard in your backyard plus 1,000 cars each weekend night would only be fun some of the time). After nearly 50 years in business, Oakley Drive-In closed and was later demolished, to be replaced with a mixed use business development.

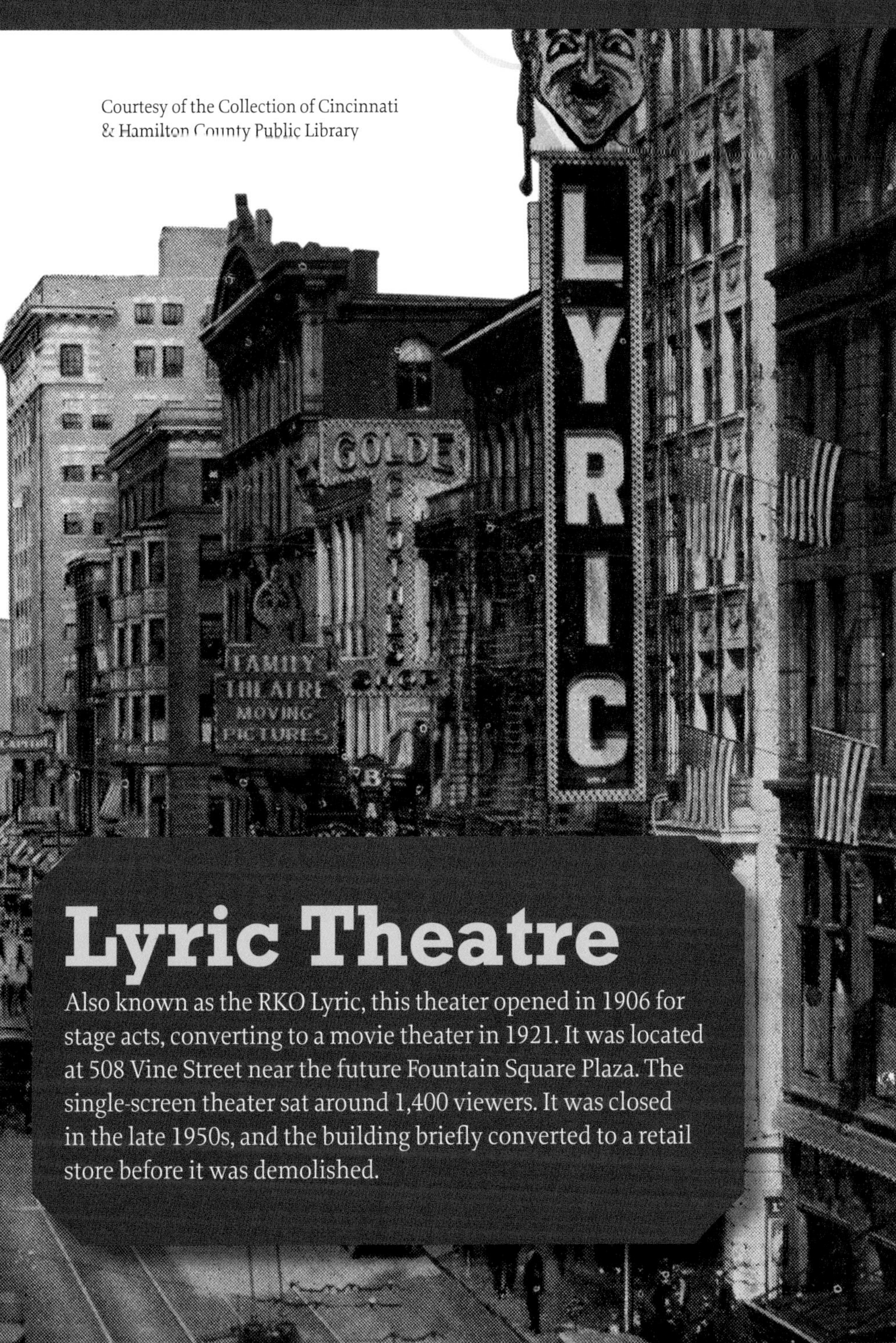

Courtesy of the Collection of Cincinnati & Hamilton County Public Library

Lyric Theatre

Also known as the RKO Lyric, this theater opened in 1906 for stage acts, converting to a movie theater in 1921. It was located at 508 Vine Street near the future Fountain Square Plaza. The single-screen theater sat around 1,400 viewers. It was closed in the late 1950s, and the building briefly converted to a retail store before it was demolished.

NIGHTCLUBS AND MUSIC VENUES

A punk show at the Jockey Club, a burlesque act at Gayety, or maybe jazz with a few Playboy Bunnies. These were just a few options on deck for Cincinnati's nightlife. Some closed, some merely faded away, and one ended in an unforgettable tragedy.

Beverly Hills Supper Club

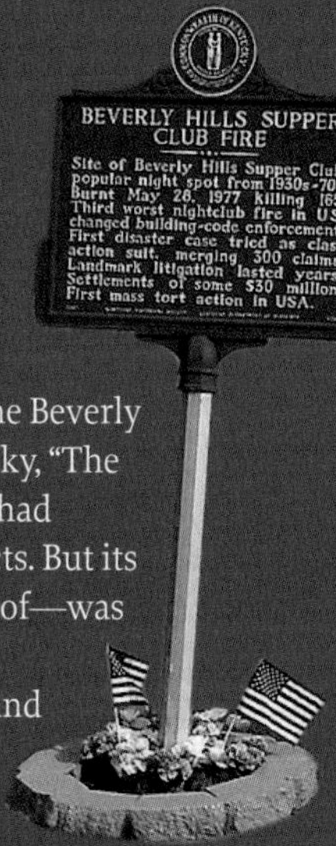

It started with a wisp of smoke and ended with the deaths of 165 people. On the night of Saturday, May 28, 1977, a raging fire destroyed the Beverly Hills Supper Club. Located in Southgate, Kentucky, "The Showplace of the Midwest" opened in 1937 and had become a destination for national performing acts. But its demise—and that of those who died under its roof—was entirely avoidable: A 1977 Kentucky state report found overcrowding, blocked emergency exits, and flammable materials among the many factors that contributed to the fire's intensity and caused the deaths. The subsequent "enterprise liability" class action lawsuit was one of the first of its kind, winning $49 million for victims and their families.

Courtesy of Wikimedia

Gayety Burlesk

From 1909 to 1970, one block of Vine Street was a hothouse of midwest burlesque. Gayety Burlesk began its life as Empress Theater (also a burlesque stage, but hiding in plain sight), changing its name in 1940 to play into the post-vaudeville bawdiness that was gaining popularity in US cities. Gayety hosted national burlesque acts in its heyday. But by 1970, with its best years behind it, the club had succumbed to the momentum of downtown development. It was demolished, eventually making way for an expanded Main Library.

Courtesy of the Collection of Cincinnati & Hamilton County Public Library

The Playboy Club

When the Playboy nightclub chain opened nationwide starting in the 1960s, it gave visitors a chance to hobnob with a waitstaff of real-life Bunnies. Cincinnati's location, at Seventh and Walnut streets downtown, opened in 1964 and ran until 1983. (The chain itself lasted all the way up to 1991.) In its 20 years downtown, the club brought a little glam to the Queen City, and gave local jazz musicians such as the Engel Trio, Mary Ellen Tanner (from WLWT's *The Bob Braun Show*) and the Dee Felice Band the chance to work alongside national acts like Sammy Davis, Jr., and Mel Torme.

Courtesy of Getty Images

Swiss Garden

Swiss Garden opened in 1925 to much hype: A two-page spread in the *Enquirer* advertised all the local products, services, and vendors that guests could expect, from Vim Ginger Ale De Luxe to a genuine Baldwin piano turning out dance music. Owners Minnie and Frank Lohman built a stage that featured jazz and dance orchestras. (Saturday night shows were broadcast at 11:00 p.m. on 700 WLW.) And then there were the manicured gardens, inviting guests to stroll and linger in the night air. It was quite a party, but by 1935 the business and building were gone. The crash of 1929—not to mention Prohibition—took its toll, and Swiss Garden was never quite the same.

Jockey Club

It was a brief but glorious run: In the six years that Jockey Club operated at 633 York Street in Newport, Kentucky, it was easily the best connected punk club in greater Cincinnati history, hosting such legendary bands as the Ramones, Hüsker Dü, Minor Threat, Dead Kennedys, and The Replacements. It was 1982, and a short-term closure of Bogart's had left a hole in the local music scene. Hallman "Shorty" Mincey stepped in with the Jockey Club. He and his crew of punk devotees (who saw Shorty as a "disapproving dad") operated it in the spirit of New York's legendary CBGB punk club. But it was not to last: Shorty sold the club in 1988, but not before he gave a generation of locals a taste of a global music movement.

Courtesy of Amy Brownlee

Southgate House

Newport businessman Ross Raleigh opened Southgate House in 1976 in an historic Newport mansion, and hosted hundreds of regional and national music acts over the next 35 years. In 2011, an abrupt family ownership shift led to Raleigh's departure; the 1812 riverfront building remained a concert venue and was renamed Thompson House (an ode to former resident John T. Thompson, inventor of the "Tommy Gun"). Raleigh moved his operation a few blocks south, opening the Southgate House Revival in the decommissioned, Civil War-era Grace Methodist Episcopal Church.

Sudsy Malone's Rock 'n Roll Laundry & Bar

Sudsy Malone's in Corryville was a fixture on the 1980s and '90s Short Vine punk and indie music scenes, a kid brother to the larger Bogart's. It was also, as promised, a laundromat and bar, so patrons could take care of important errands while catching a show. Though Sudsy's had a devoted following, it closed in 2008 and its building was demolished in 2020.

Pike's Opera House

Though its lifespan was nowhere near present day living memory, Pike's Opera House had such a spectacular demise that it cannot be left out of any list of Cincinnati's lost treasures. Construction started in 1857 on the grand, five-story building, which was situated on Fourth Street between Walnut and Vine Streets. But on March 22, 1866, a gas leak in the theater caused an explosion that destroyed the building (and took out the *Cincinnati Enquirer* offices next door). Astonishingly, no one was killed. The burned out building stood for two years before it was finally replaced with the marvelous (and also long-lost) Sinton Hotel.

Courtesy of the Collection of Cincinnati & Hamilton County Public Library

SKATING AND BOWLING

Nothing to do? You could always count on a bowling alley or skating/roller rink to provide you and your friends with a fun night out. There was Glenn Schmidt's "playtorium" in Newport (which really did have something for everyone, from bowling to gambling). Or, briefly, you could even partake in some indoor ice skating in the art deco wonder of the Netherland Plaza Hotel.

Glenn Schmidt's

Newport's "playtorium," as it was known, was a bowling alley, casino, bar, and restaurant, all in one. Glenn Schmidt's menu was "superbly prepared and served in the Kentucky manner," whatever that may mean. Fried chicken was certainly part of the deal, but you could also get barbecue, prime rib, and retro hits like chicken livers and au gratin potatoes. The site is now the Newport Syndicate banquet hall, which took over in 1995.

Courtesy of Pixabay

Del-Fair Lanes

It was billed as "the smartest cocktail lounge in the Price Hill area," and as bowling alleys went, it was fairly fancy: a 12-lane floor, electronic scorekeeping (oh la la), and a full dining menu, including fried chicken every day—Del-Fair had the works. It was even hopping on Sunday mornings: Back in the day, you could get three games and a breakfast for just $2.25.

Courtesy of the Collection of Cincinnati & Hamilton County Public Library

RECA Roller Rink

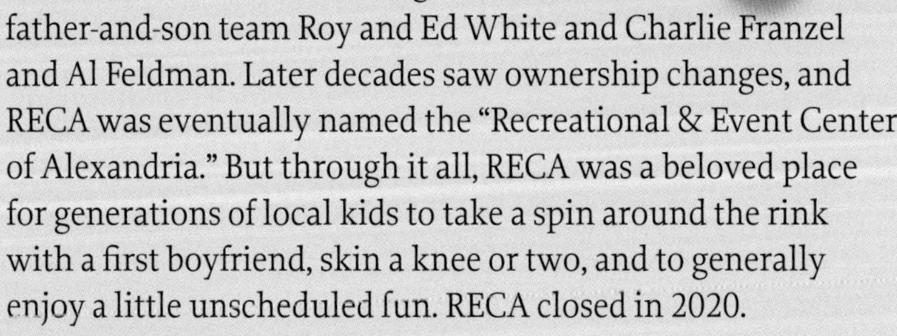

Opened in 1958 on Viewpoint Drive, just off of Alexandria Pike in Alexandria, Kentucky, the RECA Roller Rink was an acronym for the names of the founding owners, father-and-son team Roy and Ed White and Charlie Franzel and Al Feldman. Later decades saw ownership changes, and RECA was eventually named the "Recreational & Event Center of Alexandria." But through it all, RECA was a beloved place for generations of local kids to take a spin around the rink with a first boyfriend, skin a knee or two, and to generally enjoy a little unscheduled fun. RECA closed in 2020.

Courtesy of Pixabay

Netherland Ice Rink

The Netherland Plaza Hotel was built to be admired. Opened in 1931 with elaborate art deco design and luxe materials like French Fleur de Peche marble and Rookwood Pottery tiles—not to mention all those gold-plated mirrors—the hotel site eventually featured seven different restaurants and a vibrant shopping arcade. So when the Continental Room opened on the Mezzanine level, its indoor ice rink fit the bill nicely. Along with many of the hotel's other flourishes that were eventually covered up or stripped away, the ice rink was removed in the 1960s. Thankfully, current ownership has embraced the hotel's history and restored many of these original features. They haven't, however, brought back the rink—not yet, anyway.

Courtesy of Pixabay

SPORTS TEAMS AND VENUES

There's baseball, of course, and football, too. And college sports galore. But the Cincinnati of the past was home to big-league hockey and basketball, and we had the fields, tracks, stadiums, and arenas to prove it. Generations of fans have grown up with the likes of Crosley Field and Cincinnati Gardens as the center of their sporting lives.

Crosley Field

In 1934, business was good at Crosley Radio. Founder Powel Crosley Jr. bought the then struggling Cincinnati Reds. Team President Larry MacPhail suggested that their Redland Field, located at the intersection of Western Avenue and Findlay Street, be renamed in Crosley's honor. As owner, Crosley oversaw many changes to the Queensgate park, including installing the league's first lights for night games in 1935. Later in 1938, Crosley added covered upper decks along the first and third base lines, which increased capacity to just shy of 30,000 seats. In 1970, the Reds moved to downtown's larger Riverfront Stadium and Crosley Field was demolished in 1972.

Courtesy of Getty Images

Latonia Racecourse

In its time, Latonia Racecourse gave Churchill Downs a run for its money. After that venue's first wildly successful Kentucky Derby in 1875, Northern Kentucky built its own take on thoroughbred racing in 1883, complete with a four-hundred-foot-wide grandstand, landscaped infield, man-made lagoon, and eventually a large clubhouse. By the 20th century, auto racing had come to Latonia as well, and it even hosted early air shows. Latonia was sold in 1919 to the Churchill Downs owners, eventually becoming a casualty of the Great Depression, hosting its last race in 1939. It was later sold to Standard Oil Ohio, which demolished the building during World War II.

Courtesy of the Collection of Cincinnati & Hamilton County Public Library

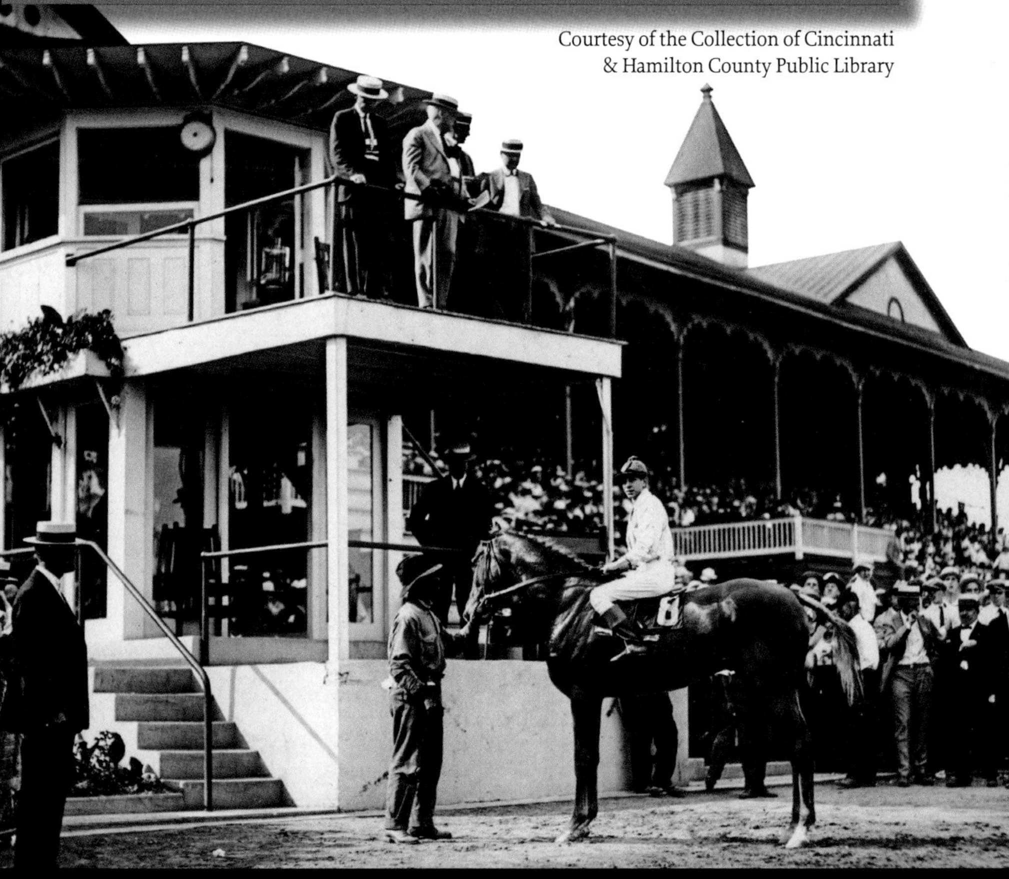

Cincinnati Royals

For 15 short years, Cincinnati was a basketball town. Sure, the Crosstown Shootout has been a concern since 1927 (played annually since 1946). But from 1957 until 1971, the Cincinnati Royals were our own pro team, lighting up the court at Cincinnati Gardens and setting records across the NBA. In the 1960s, Jerry Lucas and Oscar Robertson helped make the Royals a winning team. (Both players were honored in 1964: Oscar Robertson was named the NBA's most valuable player and Jerry Lucas was named Rookie of the Year.) By the late 1960s, however, the Royals began to decline, and by 1971, the franchise moved and eventually became the Kansas City Kings. In 1985, the Kings moved to Sacramento, where they remain today.

Cincinnati Stingers

Cincinnati's hockey scene had a brush with the big leagues: From 1975 to 1979, the Cincinnati Stingers were part of the World Hockey Association (itself a short-lived national league that hoped to rival the NHL). Playing at Riverfront Coliseum (now Heritage Bank Center), they qualified for the playoffs twice in their four major seasons, finished second in their division in 1976–77, and turned out two future Hall-of-Famers: Mike Gartner and Mark Messier. When the WHA folded in 1979, the Stingers transferred to the minor (and also now defunct) Central Hockey League for their final season.

Cincinnati Gardens

For some, Cincinnati Gardens is synonymous with the Crosstown Shootout. For others, the Cincinnati Royals come to mind. The luckiest among us might remember seeing the Beatles there in 1964, or one of Elvis Presley's two early 1970s shows. In its nearly 70 years as an indoor arena, Cincinnati Gardens played host to countless major- and minor-league games, concerts, boxing matches, and even the occasional monster truck rally. It fell out of mainstream use in the early 2000s, and after a long search for new ownership, the city demolished the iconic Bond Hill building in 2018. You can still see the original sign at Camp Washington's American Sign Museum.

The Palace of the Fans

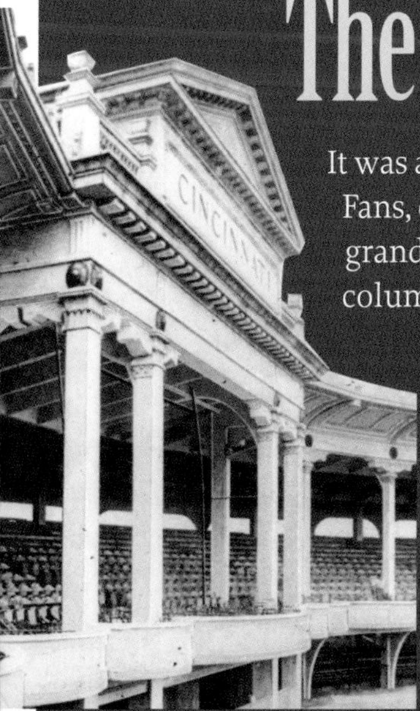

It was a nice idea, anyway. The Palace of the Fans, elaborately designed with a neoclassical grandstand and hand-carved, wooden Corinthian columns (a gutsy choice, as its predecessor, League Park, had burned to the ground in 1900) was the brainchild of Reds owner John Brush. Yet it seemed outmoded even on its 1902 Opening Day; its peers, the likes of Forbes Field and Comiskey Park, were modern monuments to stone and steel. In the end, the Palace of the Fans lasted just nine years before it was dismantled after the last game of 1911 and replaced with Redland Field in time for the 1912 season.

Courtesy of the Collection of Cincinnati & Hamilton County Public Library

RIVERFRONT STADIUM

Riverfront Stadium was Cincinnati's entry into the world of spacey sports arenas. Built to replace the much smaller Crosley Field, Riverfront was modern—and most importantly—multi-purpose: For many years it housed both the Reds and the Bengals. (The seats and field could be reconfigured for baseball or football, as needed.) It was at Riverfront Stadium where the Reds enjoyed their "Big Red Machine" era, when they dominated the National League for nearly 10 years and won two World Series titles (plus one more in 1990). The Bengals also set records at Riverfront and had two Super Bowl appearances. Riverfront was demolished in 2002 and replaced with the Great American Ballpark.

Courtesy of the Collection of Cincinnati & Hamilton County Public Library

Oakley Race Course

It lasted just 16 years, but the course was known for thoroughbred horse racing, which had recently taken off around the region at Latonia Racecourse and further south, at Churchill Downs. Originally named the Gentlemen's Full-Mile Racing Park, the Oakley course opened in 1889 west of the B&O Railroad Line and had a large and distinctive double-domed grandstand. Thanks to a state law outlawing betting, the course closed in 1905, and the Cincinnati Milling Machine Company (later Milacron) built its Oakley factory on the site.

River Downs

The "Coney Island Racetrack" opened in the summer of 1925 on the banks of the Ohio River and was nearly destroyed 12 years later by the Great Flood of 1937 (still the worst Ohio River flood on record). Renamed River Downs upon its reopening, the track was known for its 8,500-seat, open-air grandstand overlooking the Ohio River, reconstructed from the original after the 1988 season. After decades of races (and more flooding, this time in 1997), River Downs was sold in 2011; the grandstand was demolished in 2013 and the site now houses the Belterra Park Gaming & Entertainment Center.

Courtesy of the Collection of Cincinnati & Hamilton County Public Library

RETAIL

Courtesy of the Collection of Cincinnati & Hamilton County Public Library

{RETAIL}

Cincinnati's retail history is in many ways the story of a changing global economy. As with other cities large and small, we saw our localized retail first replaced by suburban big-box stores, and then by online shopping. Over the course of the 20th and 21st centuries, we went from walking around the corner to driving to a parking lot to never leaving our couches. So it may come as no surprise that there are many lost retail treasures on this list, from downtown's grande dame department stores—many of which evolved from more humble dry goods stores—to local shops that gave neighborhoods their unique character.

Courtesy of the Collection of Cincinnati & Hamilton County Public Library

DEPARTMENT STORES AND SHOPPING MALLS

"One-stop shopping" is a concept that drove much of the retail development in the United States over the late-19th and early-20th centuries. Enterprising shop owners looked to lure customers through their doors and then wow them with an incredible array of products, from clothing to jewelry to appliances, all under one roof—like a casino, but with a shoe department. The idea stuck and evolved (or devolved, depending on your perspective) into the shopping mall, which hitched a ride on mid-century car culture and relocated the shopping away from downtown. The requisite acreage of surface parking lots would come to characterize suburban living. But many Cincinnatians still remember the downtown shopping experience—an event that required one's best outfit—and the sense of excitement and possibility that went with it.

Courtesy of Amy Brownlee

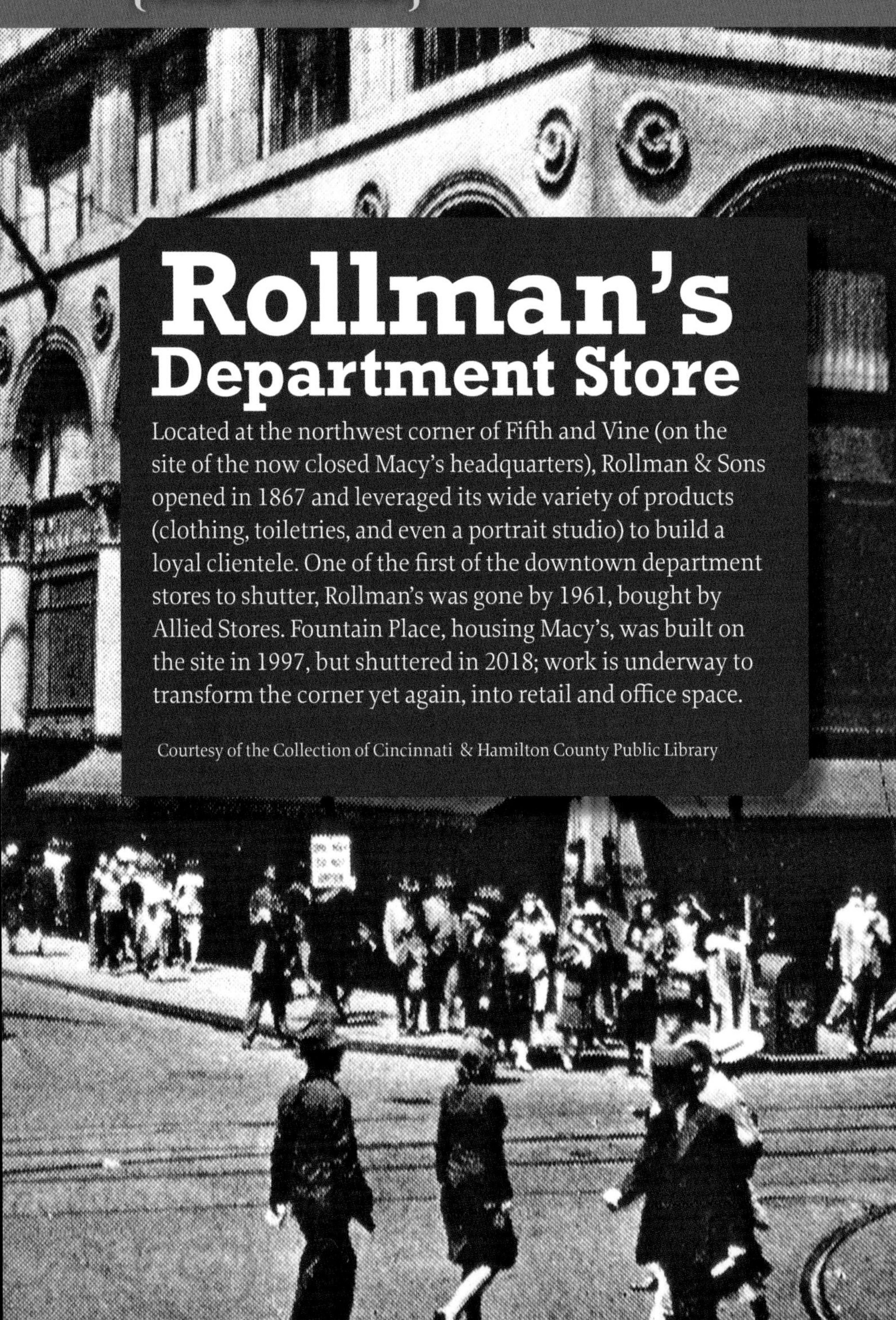

Rollman's Department Store

Located at the northwest corner of Fifth and Vine (on the site of the now closed Macy's headquarters), Rollman & Sons opened in 1867 and leveraged its wide variety of products (clothing, toiletries, and even a portrait studio) to build a loyal clientele. One of the first of the downtown department stores to shutter, Rollman's was gone by 1961, bought by Allied Stores. Fountain Place, housing Macy's, was built on the site in 1997, but shuttered in 2018; work is underway to transform the corner yet again, into retail and office space.

Courtesy of the Collection of Cincinnati & Hamilton County Public Library

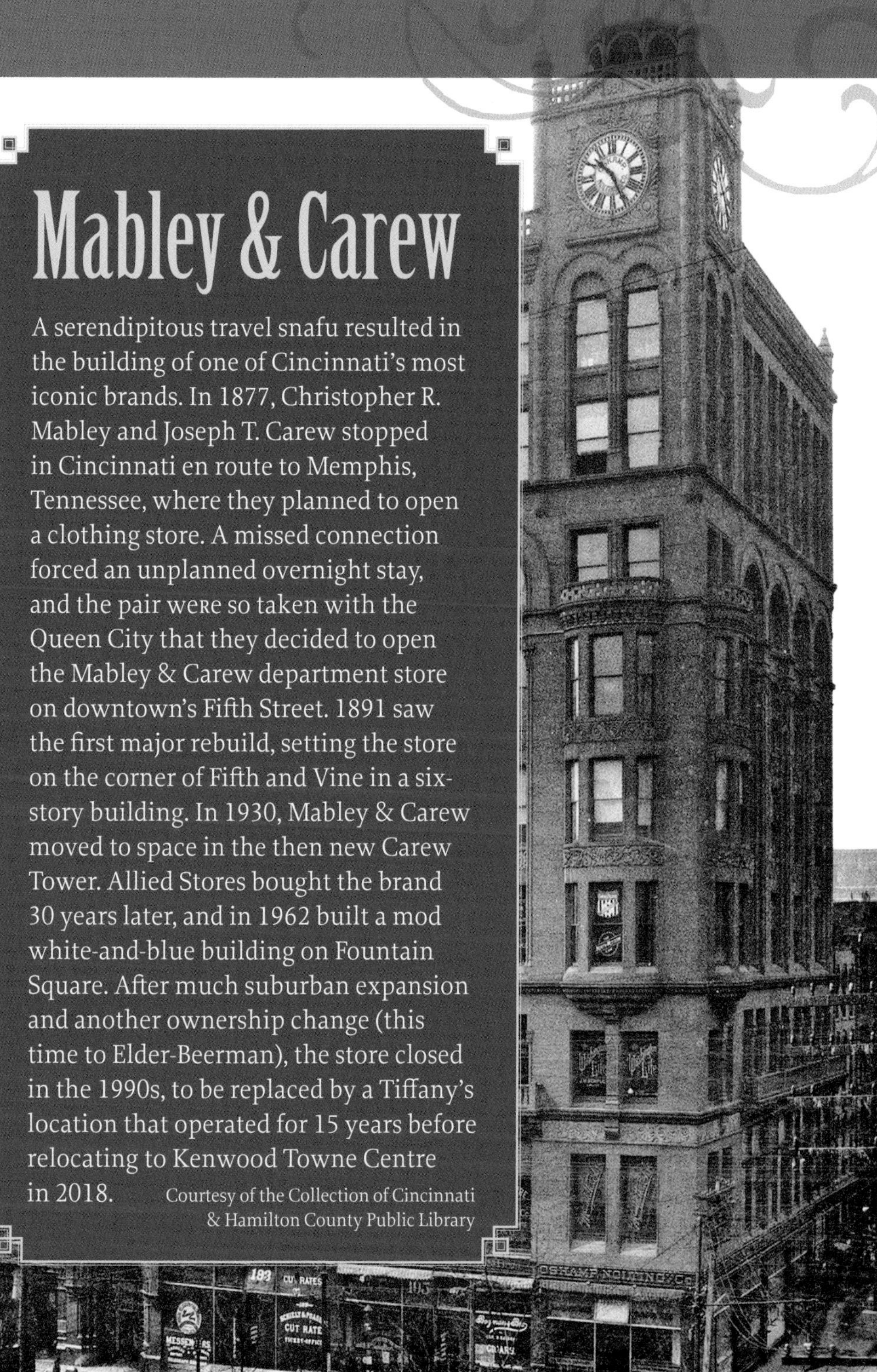

Mabley & Carew

A serendipitous travel snafu resulted in the building of one of Cincinnati's most iconic brands. In 1877, Christopher R. Mabley and Joseph T. Carew stopped in Cincinnati en route to Memphis, Tennessee, where they planned to open a clothing store. A missed connection forced an unplanned overnight stay, and the pair were so taken with the Queen City that they decided to open the Mabley & Carew department store on downtown's Fifth Street. 1891 saw the first major rebuild, setting the store on the corner of Fifth and Vine in a six-story building. In 1930, Mabley & Carew moved to space in the then new Carew Tower. Allied Stores bought the brand 30 years later, and in 1962 built a mod white-and-blue building on Fountain Square. After much suburban expansion and another ownership change (this time to Elder-Beerman), the store closed in the 1990s, to be replaced by a Tiffany's location that operated for 15 years before relocating to Kenwood Towne Centre in 2018.

Courtesy of the Collection of Cincinnati & Hamilton County Public Library

Pogue's

Another local dry goods store upgrade, Pogue's was founded in 1863 by Irish immigrant brothers Henry and Samuel Pogue, and it grew to become a high-end shopping destination. The flagship store building, designed by Samuel Hannaford in 1916, opened in the fashionable shopping district on Fourth Street between Race and Vine Streets. The shop expanded in 1930 and had direct access to the shiny new Carew Tower Arcade and a full complement of amenities: Generations of Cincinnatians visited the Pogue's Tea Room, Camargo Room restaurant, and the famous Ice Cream Bridge, which opened in 1964 and spanned the Carew Tower Arcade. Like other department stores of its generation, Pogue's expanded into the suburbs in the 1950s, and by 1961 was sold to Associated Dry Goods (affiliated with Lord & Taylor). The Pogue's name eventually was dropped in the 1980s.

Courtesy of the Collection of Cincinnati & Hamilton County Public Library

Swallen's

If you wanted to buy it, Swallen's probably had it. Opened in 1948, the Cincinnati-based discount store sold everything from clothing to cameras—even pets. Wilbur "Pat" Swallen opened a small shop in his garage on Red Bank Road after World War II—expanding to a Fairfax storefront in 1953—and Swallen's soon grew to become a local institution. Contemporary consumers are unmoved by Walmarts in every city, but Swallen's was doing something new in mid- century America by offering value-priced items in just about every category imaginable. By 1995, however, amid stalling sales, Swallen's had filed for bankruptcy and closed all of its locations.

COPPIN'S Department Store

In 1873, John R. Coppin opened the California Dry Goods Co. at what is now the corner of Seventh Street and Madison Avenue in Covington, Kentucky. After more than 30 years of success, Coppin commissioned a new seven-story building in 1907 and leveled up his own offerings to make his store the biggest and best in the region. After more than 100 years in business, Coppin's closed in 1977, its building sitting empty for more than 10 years before the city of Covington moved to save it. You can still visit Coppin's. In fact, you can stay over: The building has been lovingly restored and now houses the 114-room Hotel Covington. An on-site restaurant was named in the store's honor.

Swifton Shopping Center

Billed as a "city within a city" when it opened in 1956, Swifton Shopping Center was Cincinnati's first shopping mall, with a new Rollman's department store at its heart (Mabley took over the space just a few years later). Swifton's construction and success ushered in a retail revolution in the region, with a mall built in nearly every major suburb throughout the next decade. But due in part to that growing competition, Swifton began to fail as early as the 1970s, and by the 1980s it was half empty. The slow decline continued and eventually the 25-acre site was sold to the city; it was renamed "MidPointe Crossing" in 2019 and is on track for eventual mixed-use development.

Shillito's Department Store

When John Shillito expanded his dry goods store in 1830, Shillito's became Cincinnati's first department store. In 1877, the shop occupied a new building on Seventh and Race, featuring a six-floor atrium and interior skylight dome. Shillito's evolved into a stylish emporium with fine jewelry and linens, designer clothing, and a fur salon. (The shop also eventually had TVs and vacuum cleaners.) It was sold to the Lazarus family in 1928, who oversaw a 1937 art deco makeover for the flagship building: a shell of limestone, granite, and marble wrapped around the original brick facade. After much suburban expansion in the 1960s and 1970s, Shillito's eventually became part of Macy's. The original building is now home to the Lofts at Shillito Place.

Courtesy of the Collection of Cincinnati & Hamilton County Public Library

Eilerman's Department Store

Starting in the early 1900s (some sources say late 1800s), Eilerman's was the top shop for clothing for men and boys in Northern Kentucky. With locations in Newport and Covington (and even a Lima, Ohio, store), Eilerman's was known for its sleek and modern merchandising and elaborate window displays. Like many department stores of its generation, though, Eilerman's went extinct in the 1960s. The Newport building is now home to Tailor Lofts, named in honor of its clothing store history.

Courtesy of Wikimedia

Gidding-Jenny

Though slightly smaller than some of its department store peers, Gidding-Jenny was no less elegant. J. M. Gidding & Co. opened on west Fourth Street in 1907 selling menswear; the building sported an unrivaled facade trimmed in a (still visible) Rookwood Pottery relief of colorful fruit and flowers. Womens' shop the Jenny Co. opened in 1922 and moved next door to Gidding in 1939 (right around the time its famous "Milbron" dress hit the market). The shops operated in tandem until 1961, when Genesco (formerly General Shoe Co.) acquired Gidding in 1961 and Jenny in 1962, and then merged the two. Gidding-Jenny outfitted smart Cincinnatians for the next 30 years until struggling sales forced its closure in 1995.

Courtesy of Amy Brownlee

Western Woods Mall

Western Woods Mall opened on Glenway Avenue with an anchor Shillito's store in 1963, and the neighboring single-screen Western Woods Cinema opened just a few years later. The mall went above and beyond typical retail stores; shoppers may remember Western Woods Barber Shop, a Thriftway supermarket, and Gallaher Drug. By the 1980s, however, stores began pulling out or closing altogether. Much of the mall was vacant by the time it was finally demolished in the 1990s.

Courtesy of the Collection of Cincinnati & Hamilton County Public Library

Forest Fair Mall

Courtesy of Wikimedia

It may still be standing, but this ghost mall is a shadow of its former self. When it opened in the late 1980s, Forest Fair Mall (later called Cincinnati Mills) was the second-largest mall in the state and popular with shoppers but immediately plagued with money troubles. With its pastel-colored interior, movie theater, and mesmerizing "ball machine" sculpture, Forest Fair was the image of 1990s suburbia. But after years of decline, the mall is now nearly empty except for a few remaining tenants and a small army of mall-walkers.

RETAIL STORES

DOW'S DRUG STORE

Dow's Drug at Seventh and Race was a sight to behold. But the least exceptional thing about these shops was their beauty. After Cora Dow became one of the first women to graduate from Cincinnati College of Pharmacy in the late 1880s, she eventually took over and expanded her father's drug store business. Dow fought for increasing women's involvement in the industry, from more female drug clerks to more female customers, and designed her 11 store locations to offer the very best, from beauty products to pharmaceuticals to ice cream.

Courtesy of the Collection of Cincinnati & Hamilton County Public Library

McDevitt's Men's Shop

McDevitt's Men's Shop was opened in Walnut Hills in 1896 by James and Joseph McDevitt, soon after expanding to multiple locations in the neighborhood. Its most notable address was the iconic Paramount Building at Peebles' Corner, a busy shopping and entertainment district now listed in the National Register of Historic Places. For decades, McDevitt's outfitted smart Cincinnatians in everything from suits to suspenders, but eventually closed in 1970 as shopping malls drew customers out to the suburbs. The building survived, and is now a mixed-use project dubbed Paramount Square & Trevarren Flats.

Courtesy of Amy Brownlee

JOHNNY'S TOYS

Ask any local 1990s kid about Johnny's Toys and they'll probably shout something about the birthday key. Each year, if you were a member of the Birthday Club, you received in the mail a colorful card taped to a tiny key. That key granted you entrance to the Birthday Castle in the back corner of the Latonia, Kentucky, store, where you then selected the tchotchke of your choice. It was a genius marketing ploy, and it lent a little extra magic to local birthdays until the store shuttered in 2009. Repair shop Tech Castle now inhabits the old store space (castle and all) and has revived and reinvented the tradition by making 3D-printed keys in the store.

CLOSSON'S

(The A. B. Closson's Jr. Co.)

For most of its lifetime, Closson's was a fixture on downtown's Fourth Street. Founded in 1866 on West Fourth as an art gallery, the shop expanded in the 1920s to sell furnishings and textiles, moving to 421 Race Street in 1933. If there was a Closson's Golden Age, it was the 1960s: In 1964, art philanthropist Phyllis Weston took over the art gallery, where she championed local artists like John Ruthven, and the shop moved again in 1966 to a 37,000-square-foot store at Fourth and Race. The final move was to Oakley in 2003; Closson's closed its doors in 2010 after 144 years in business.

Courtesy of the Collection of Cincinnati & Hamilton County Public Library

Courtesy of Pixabay

Alms and Doepke

Spread along a full block of Central Parkway, the former Alms and Doepke Dry Goods Company building remains a formidable presence on the edge of Over-the-Rhine. Designed by Samuel Hannaford and built in or around 1878, the brick structure housed one of the area's leading dry goods outfits. Alms and Doepke was founded on lower Main Street in 1865 by brothers William H. and Frederick H. Alms and William F. Doepke, all three of whom had just finished serving in the Union Army. The firm continued to grow, serving an expanding Over-the-Rhine throughout the late-19th and early-20th centuries. The shop closed in 1955, and its headquarters building now houses Hamilton County Job and Family Services.

Courtesy of Wikimedia, Greg Hume

Newstedt-Loring Andrews

In 1805, enterprising pioneer Alexander McGraw started selling pocket watches to steamboat passengers visiting the fledgling Ohio River city of Cincinnati (which had been settled just a handful of years earlier). That hussle eventually became the Newstedt-Loring Andrews jewelry store, which had locations along downtown's Fourth Street throughout the 19th and 20th centuries. In 1996, the shop moved to Hyde Park Square, where it flourished until its 2019 closing.

Loesch Hardware

Loesch Hardware opened on Oakley's Madison Road in 1924 and fast became a local landmark and home base for East Side do-it-yourself-ers. Greg Gordon closed the shop in 2015 after more than 90 years in the neighborhood, citing a loss of local industry business. Gordon ran the shop for 33 years and was just the fourth owner since Loesch's opening. The building's new tenant is fitting: It's now home to Oakley Paint & Glass, an affiliate of Cincinnati Color Company, which has been a local name since 1928.

Courtesy of Pixabay

WIZARD RECORDS & TAPES

Cincinnatians who knew Corryville's Short Vine as it was in the 1980s and early 1990s will remember Wizard for the repository of culture, community, and cool that it was. The shop sat on the same street as Bogart's and Sudsy Malone's, two beloved local music venues (Sudsy's is, unfortunately, on this Lost Treasures list). Former Wizard owner-manager John Mark James remembers that there was "something magical" about the store, which attracted musicians, students, and kids from the 'burbs, all of whom flocked there to dig through crates of old LPs, find out what good shows were playing, or pass the time while their band was being sound-checked.

Marboro Books

Richard Wenstrup opened a Marboro Books branch at 516 Vine Street in 1964, eventually landing on Sixth Street in a Terrace Hilton storefront. There were already a few established book shops downtown, but Marboro was doing something different, selling pop art posters, LPs, buttons, and even issues of alt papers like the *Village Voice* alongside its stock of unstuffy paperbacks. Though it closed in 1969, the Marboro ethos continued when Wenstrup purchased Kidd's Booksellers and added his own counterculture spin to the established shop's more conventional offerings.

James Book Store

Established in 1831, James Book Store billed itself as "The Oldest Bookstore West of the Alleghenies." According to the Mercantile Library, James Book Store's history dates back to a pair of printer/booksellers named Joseph and Uriah Pierson James, who journeyed to the city by stagecoach and canal boat. The shop was open well into the late 20th century.

Kidd's Booksellers

Located at 626 Vine Street (with a branch in the Carew Tower Arcade), Kidd's Booksellers formerly had locations on Pearl Street and later Main Street and was long-established as a purveyor of books old and new, as well as office supplies, stationery, and a "whole floor of children's books." Marboro Books's owner Richard Wenstrup brought an underground element to Kidd's when he bought it in the late 1960s: He literally sold his stock of alt books and magazines from the shop's basement.

Courtesy of Pixabay

HOTELS AND MOTELS

Before chain brands made the hotel-staying experience somewhat bland (though, admittedly, far more reliable and consistent), there were countless private hotels throughout the city. Many of these were very grand, and put Cincinnati on the map with travelers from all over the world. In an effort to distinguish themselves from the pack, hotels offered impressive public amenities, from rathskellers to candy shops to billiard rooms. More than anything, though, they represented an era of genteel travel culture that deserves a comeback.

Courtesy of the Collection of Cincinnati & Hamilton County Public Library

Gibson House

"500 Rooms, 500 Baths." That was the king-sized promise of Gibson House, built in 1912 overlooking the south side of the original Fountain Square esplanade (which straddled Fifth Street between Vine and Walnut Streets, just east of Carew Tower). Developing a reputation as one of the city's finest establishments, Gibson House (also known as Hotel Gibson) hosted leading figures, including John F. Kennedy, who stayed there in 1960 while campaigning for president. The hotel went out of business in 1974, and was demolished in 1977 (along with its neighbor the Albee Theater) to make way for the Westin Hotel.

Courtesy of the Collection of Cincinnati & Hamilton County Public Library

Sinton Hotel

Its prominent role in the 1919 World Series scandal is somehow not the most exceptional thing about the Sinton Hotel. Built in 1907 at the southeast corner of Fourth and Vine Streets, the spectacularly appointed hotel contained 450 guest rooms (300 were added later), and multiple dining and recreation options, including a Great Banquet Room, the Forest Glade room, the Grand Cafe, and a Ladies' Dining Room, plus The Kneipe (a basement pub), the Louis XVI Candy Shop, a coffee shop, a convention hall, and a billiard room. In spite of all this luxury, the Sinton did become notorious when members of the Chicago White Sox and the Cincinnati Reds met there with gamblers to plan the fix of the century. In 1968, the hotel was torn down and replaced with the Provident Bank Tower (now called the National City Tower).

Courtesy of the Collection of Cincinnati & Hamilton County Public Library

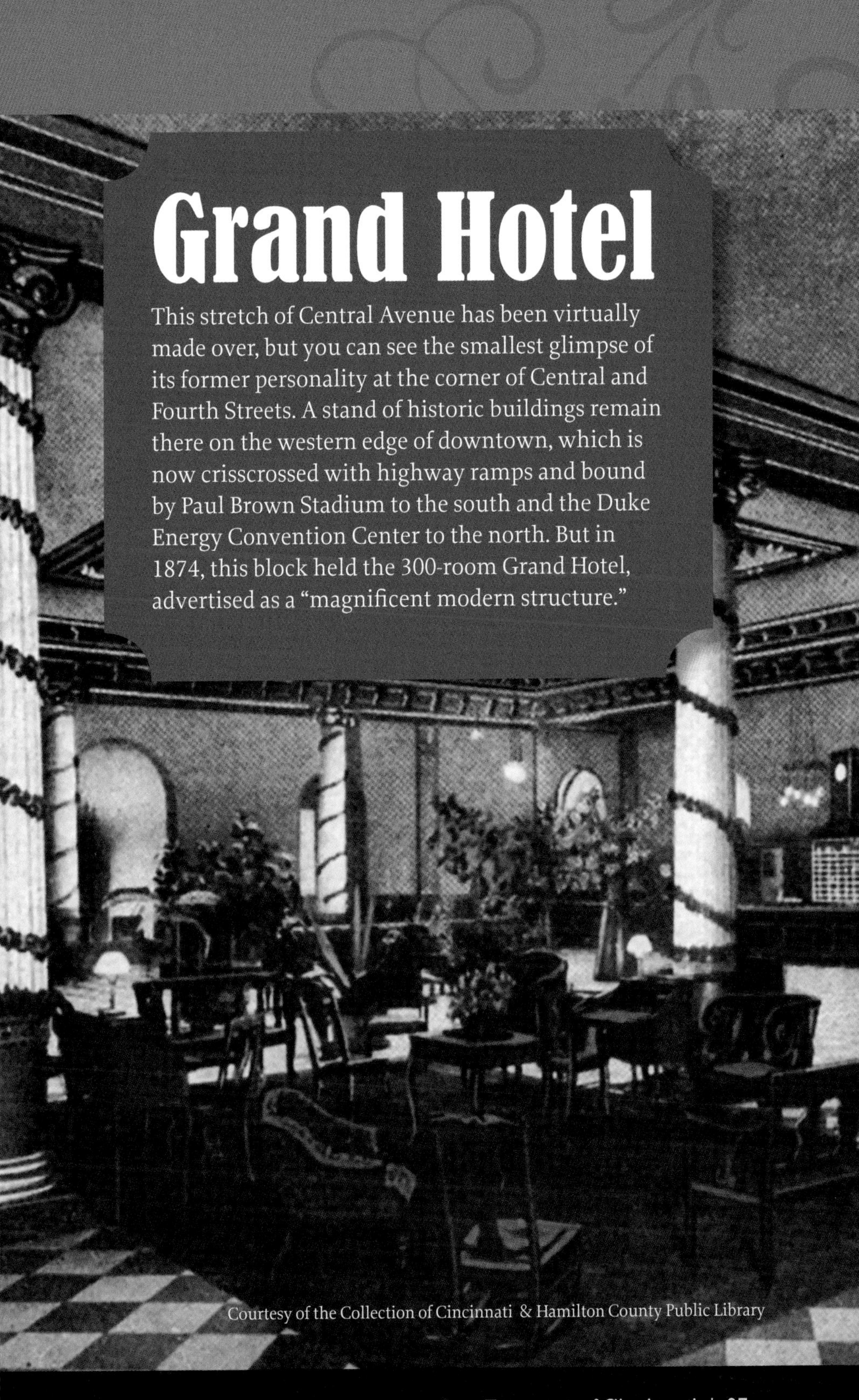

Grand Hotel

This stretch of Central Avenue has been virtually made over, but you can see the smallest glimpse of its former personality at the corner of Central and Fourth Streets. A stand of historic buildings remain there on the western edge of downtown, which is now crisscrossed with highway ramps and bound by Paul Brown Stadium to the south and the Duke Energy Convention Center to the north. But in 1874, this block held the 300-room Grand Hotel, advertised as a "magnificent modern structure."

Courtesy of the Collection of Cincinnati & Hamilton County Public Library

Dennison Hotel

This unassuming 1892 building on downtown's Main Street became a flashpoint for preservation activism when developers sought to replace the aging structure with a new office building block and preservationists saw it as an important part of the historic neighborhood's past. Designed by Samuel Hannaford's famed architectural firm, it was first used as a manufacturing center, then later in the 1930s as a hotel, and finally as affordable housing apartments. After years of court battles and protests, the Dennison was finally demolished in 2017.

Vernon Manor Hotel

The distinctive building still stands in Clifton, now used as an office building for Cincinnati Children's Medical Hospital. But its first life was as a smart urban hotel. Completed in 1924, Vernon Manor hosted visiting dignitaries and celebrities, such as President John F. Kennedy and the Beatles. Vernon Manor was known as one of the city's top-shelf hotels. Eventually the property began its decline, and it was sold in 1977, operating as low-income housing until its office space facelift in 2011.

Terrace Plaza Hotel

When it was built in 1948, it was exceedingly modern. To a post-war America, Terrace Plaza Hotel, designed by 24-year-old architect Natalie de Blois, was practically futuristic: elevators without operators, guest rooms with individual climate controls (now an industry standard), push-button convertible sofas, and a conspicuous lack of ornament in the windowless red brick facade that soared over West Sixth Street. And then there were the murals: A surreal circular wonder by Joan Miró trimmed the Gourmet Room restaurant and a witty Cincinnati-themed work by Saul Steinberg, both now at the Cincinnati Art Museum. But it was not to last. By the 1990s, after years of ownership changes and downtown depopulation, the building sat abandoned. In 2017, it was placed on the National Historic Register, but it remains empty, with its future undetermined.

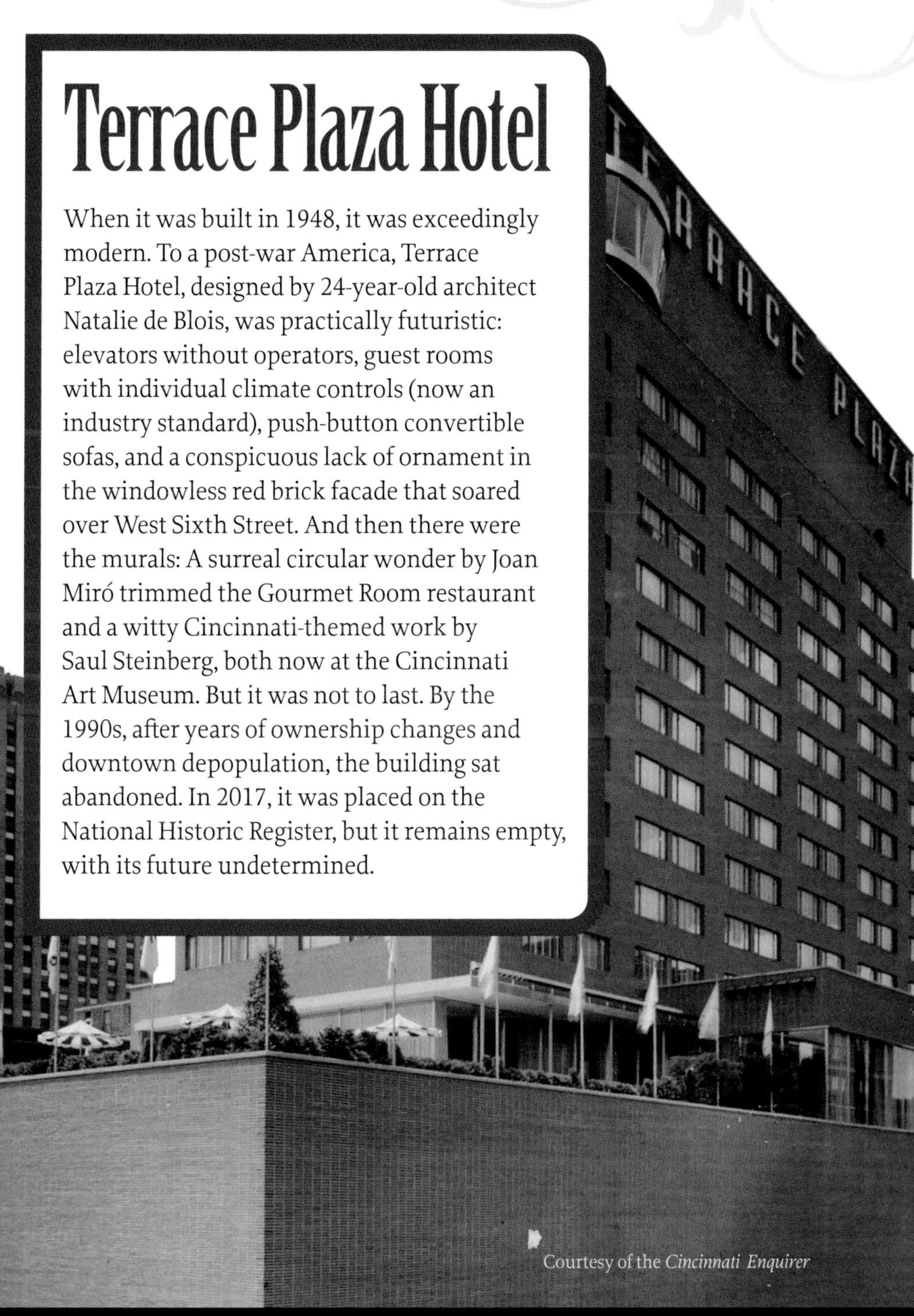

Courtesy of the *Cincinnati Enquirer*

{MEDIA}

Courtesy of the Collection of Cincinnati & Hamilton County Public Library

PRINT

Cincinnati's print media history is both intensely localized and impressively global: Many newspaper titles have reported on local news over the decades. And the *McGuffey Reader*, arguably the nation's first standardized textbook, was first printed at downtown's American Book Company.

McGuffey Readers

In 1834, William Holmes McGuffey started work on his *McGuffey Readers* from his Oxford, Ohio, home. The books, printed at Cincinnati's American Book Company, sold more than 100 million copies by the end of the century. Unlike other readers of the time, McGuffey's books were actually geared towards children, with a lighthearted tone and appearance (local artist Henry Farny contributed the realistic illustrations), compared to their more puritanical predecessors. Though *McGuffey Readers* fell out of use around the 1920s, they are actually still being printed today (in far fewer numbers). At their height, they educated countless schoolchildren and changed the face of American public education.

Images courtesy of McGuffey House and Museum, Miami University

The Independent Eye

The Independent Eye launched in response to the Vietnam War, fast developing as a discerning local voice for the world's counterculture movements. Founded in 1968 at Antioch College in Yellow Springs, Ohio, and then relocated to Cincinnati in 1969, the nonprofit paper was published by the Eye Information Center. It sought to connect its readers to issues of the day through reported and contributed articles, cartoons, literary works, and photographs. (Acclaimed *Cincinnati Post* photojournalist Melvin Grier was among their contributors.) National and international news items covered everything from women's and gay liberation to workers' rights to civil right. *The Independent Eye* was also a clearinghouse of local services and organizations like the ACLU and the UC Law Clinic. *The Independent Eye* closed up shop in 1975—incidentally, the same year as the Fall of Saigon.

"Win The World Series Sweepstakes!"

The Independent EYE

Cincinnati Paints the Town RED!

BROMLEYS WIN VICTORY--PATTY STRIKES OUT!

Courtesy of Ellen Bierhorst

The *Cincinnati Post*

Cincinnati's daily afternoon edition, the *Cincinnati Post* (originally called the *Penny Paper*) launched in 1881 and for many locals, particularly on the West Side and in Kentucky, it was the paper of record. The *Post* was known for investigative pieces and dynamic photojournalism, and constituted a crucial "second journalistic voice" in the city alongside the *Cincinnati Enquirer*. Its slow decline, delayed by a joint operating agreement with the *Enquirer* in the 1970s, picked up speed in the 1980s until the paper collapsed in stages of downsizing and layoffs. Its final print edition was on December 31, 2007.

TELEVISION

Did you know that the first daytime television talk show was made right in Cincinnati? Ruth Lyons premiered the concept in 1946, and TV never looked back. There was also *The Uncle Al Show*, which for many Cincinnati kids was their first personal experience with appearing on television (and it helped to launch the career of none other than George Clooney). Unlike the show *WKRP in Cincinnati* (see: Icons and Curiosities), these productions were actually created here by Cincinnatians for generations of local fans.

The 50/50 Club

The *50/50 Club* actually started out as just *The 50 Club*. In 1946, Ruth Lyons aired the first episode of her show concept on WLW, where a live radio broadcast captured a daily, hour-long lunch comprised of 50 women guests, hosted by Lyons herself. Three years later, she made the jump to television and expanded the show to 100 guests (hence the name change). With the move, Lyons essentially invented the daytime TV talk show, and created a national institution. Lyons, the "first lady of television," was known for her product demonstrations, songs, and special guests, and of course for her famous microphone bouquet.

Courtesy of Pixabay

The Uncle Al Show

The Uncle Al Show aired on WCPO for 35 years, making it one of the longest-running children's programs in American TV history. Part of what made *Uncle Al* different—and so memorable for so many Cincinnatians—was its audience participation: Local kids were often given stage jobs like holding puppets, or were selected to participate in show skits (native son George Clooney first appeared in 1970, playing a ship's captain). Regular *Uncle Al* characters included Pal the Dog, Lucky the Clown, and the Merry Mailman. The show filmed an estimated 15,000 episodes before its 1985 cancellation.

Past Prime Playhouse

There was *Saturday Night Live*, but first there was *Bob Shreve's Past Prime Playhouse.* One part Vaudevillian, one part cornpone Pee-wee Herman, comedian Bob Shreve got his start on country music show *Midwestern Hayride* in the early 1950s. His comedy show *Past Prime Playhouse* aired overnight on Saturdays on Channel 12 WKRC from 1974 until 1985, and its slapstick jokes and one-liners were beloved among late-night Cincinnati TV viewers. Personalities like Adam West and Morganna, the Kissing Bandit, were among guests on *PPP*. Shreve's career also intersected with at least two other Lost Treasures alums: He made frequent appearances on both *The 50/50 Club* and *The Uncle Al Show.*

{The COMMUNITY}

Courtesy of the Collection of Cincinnati & Hamilton County Public Library

{The COMMUNITY}

Many towns claim to be a "Queen City," but only Cincinnati has the real bona fides to own the title: Journalists in the early 19th century noted our then young city's role in America's westward expansion, dubbing Cincinnati the "Queen City of the West" and capturing the imagination of enterprising immigrants and would-be pioneers. The term caught on, and by the mid-1850s, Henry Wadsworth Longfellow had penned "Ode to Catawba Wine"—inspired no doubt by the case of the stuff that vineyard owner Nicholas Longworth, who was producing and distributing 100,000 bottles of sparkling Catawba wine each year, had sent to the poet. After much rhyming about the "dulcet, delicious and dreamy" wine, the poem concludes, "And this Song of the Vine, This greeting of mine, The winds and the birds shall deliver To the Queen of the West, In her garlands dressed, On the banks of the Beautiful River." The literary hat tip only endorsed what scores of settlers already knew: Cincinnati was something special, and it was here to stay.

We were the "Queen City" before much of what we know today was even built. The 1880s saw an explosion of German immigration (perhaps in part to that breathless recognition of our "garlands dressed") and with it an entire brewing industry. The neighborhood of Over-the-Rhine, with its huge collection of Italianate row houses, sprang up to support the new communities calling the city home. And as Cincinnati's urban population grew more and more dense and diverse, neighborhoods opened up throughout the basin and in the surrounding hills to meet the demand. With people come the trappings of culture and commerce: schools, factories, places of worship, hospitals, and more.

Like most places, Cincinnati is built upon its past: Items on this list represent times gone by but were often replaced with institutions that are still going strong. And then there are many places, including a host of handsome downtown buildings and structures that made our city dense, compact, and convenient, that are simply gone forever.

Images courtesy of the Collection of Cincinnati & Hamilton County Public Library

ARCHITECTURE AND BUILDINGS

Samuel Hannaford's fingerprints are all over Cincinnati. Born in England in 1835, the aspiring architect came to Cincinnati as a young boy in the 1840s, and proceeded to design (or beget, via the firm of Samuel Hannaford & Sons) some of our most noteworthy and enduring structures: Music Hall, City Hall, the Cincinnati Observatory, and many dozens more that dot our city's landscape. A remarkable number of these still stand. Others, of course, are lost.

Downtown's architectural makeup has shifted dramatically through the decades, most notably in the blocks stretching from the river and up into the West End. As the city took shape and shed its earlier rivertown skin, the landing and streets leading out of the valley were nearly completely made over from their earlier selves. Later still, as cars overtook train travel here and throughout the United States, Cincinnati became more reliant upon high-speed freeway systems. These literally plowed through our neighborhoods, and what were once lively and densely occupied communities downtown and in the West End—filled with people that were born, loved, worked, worshipped, learned, lived, and died—are now highways, stadiums, and parking lots. It's an appalling loss.

Evolution is the destiny of every locale, for better or for worse. Indeed, it was an eye towards growth that led the immigrant Hannaford to leave his mark on a young American city. His vision remains, both in brick-and-mortar buildings that still stand and in the pride of place that reminds us to build, grow, and also to preserve.

Ohio National Guard Armory

True to its name, the Ohio National Guard Armory had an imposing presence at 1439 Freeman Avenue. The fort-like structure was designed by Samuel Hannaford and built between 1886–1889, when Hannaford was also busy with the planning and construction of City Hall. (He also designed the Sisters of Mercy school and convent next door in 1898. It's now occupied by Job Corps.) The building served as the headquarters for the 1st regiment of the Ohio National Guard until 1961; it was demolished in the mid-1980s and the site now houses office and manufacturing space.

Courtesy of the Collection of Cincinnati & Hamilton County Public Library

Neave Building

Built around 1892 at the northwest corner of Fourth and Race Streets downtown, the 11-story Neave Building was an attractive local example of Chicago School architecture, which is characterized by steel frame construction, large windows, and relatively limited exterior ornamentation. (Many such buildings are considered early versions of the contemporary skyscraper.) It was eventually demolished and replaced with the Pogue's parking garage in the 1960s (later renamed Tower Place Garage). After nearly 50 years, that unsightly structure was itself torn down in 2016 to make way for a luxury apartment building.

Citizens National Bank

Built in 1906, the Citizens National Bank, later Provident Bank, was yet another Samuel Hannaford design gracing the city's urban landscape. It stood at Fourth and Main Streets, on the southeast corner. (The Neoclassical Cincinnati Gas & Electric Company Building, now the Duke Energy Building, was built across the street 20 years later.) The 1970s brought many changes to downtown's built environment, and the full-scale replacement of this corner was one of them; you'll now find the streamlined Omnicare Center, a creation of architectural firm Skidmore, Owings and Merrill.

Perrin Building

The intersection of Fifth and Race Streets downtown was transformed many times over during the 20th century (only the Netherland Plaza Hotel remains; it has held down the southeast corner since its 1931 opening). And for nearly 80 years, the splendid Perrin Building rose tall just across the street. Built in the 1880s, it exemplified Cincinnati's grand downtown towers: Many features, such as the stacked arch windows, also appear in the more famous Gwynne Building, which still stands at Sixth and Main Streets. The Perrin Building was torn down in 1969. In 2015, data science company 84.51° built its massive headquarters building on the former site.

Images courtesy of the Collection of Cincinnati & Hamilton County Public Library

Burnet House

Despite being one of the world's finest hotels of its time, Burnet House's two claims-to-fame were the Lincoln visits. He stayed at the 340-room hotel twice: first in 1859 while campaigning for the Ohio Republican Party and again in 1861 as he made his inaugural journey to Washington. President Lincoln, newly elected at the time, stood at the Burnet House balcony and spoke against slavery. The Civil War began just two months later. The hotel remained in the limelight for decades but eventually declined and then closed; it was demolished in 1926. Just two years later, the Union Central Life company built a Neoclassical Revival-style annex over the spot, which is now the City Club Apartments.

Eden Park Reservoir

Courtesy of the Library of Congress

In the 1860s, Cincinnati barely had enough water to get its nearly 200,000 residents through a single day. The city was in desperate need of a much larger and more reliable water reservoir. Completed in 1875 on the former site of Nicholas Longworth's failed "Garden of Eden" Catawba wine vineyard, the 14-acre Eden Park reservoir increased the city's water storage capacity to 100 million gallons (up from around 25 million). Though it was removed in the 1960s, the project's spirit—and many of its actual components—remains. The Station No. 7 and Stand Pipe (designed by Samuel Hannaford) stand in Eden Park along with part of the original dam, and the former reservoir surface is now the Mirror Lake reflecting pool.

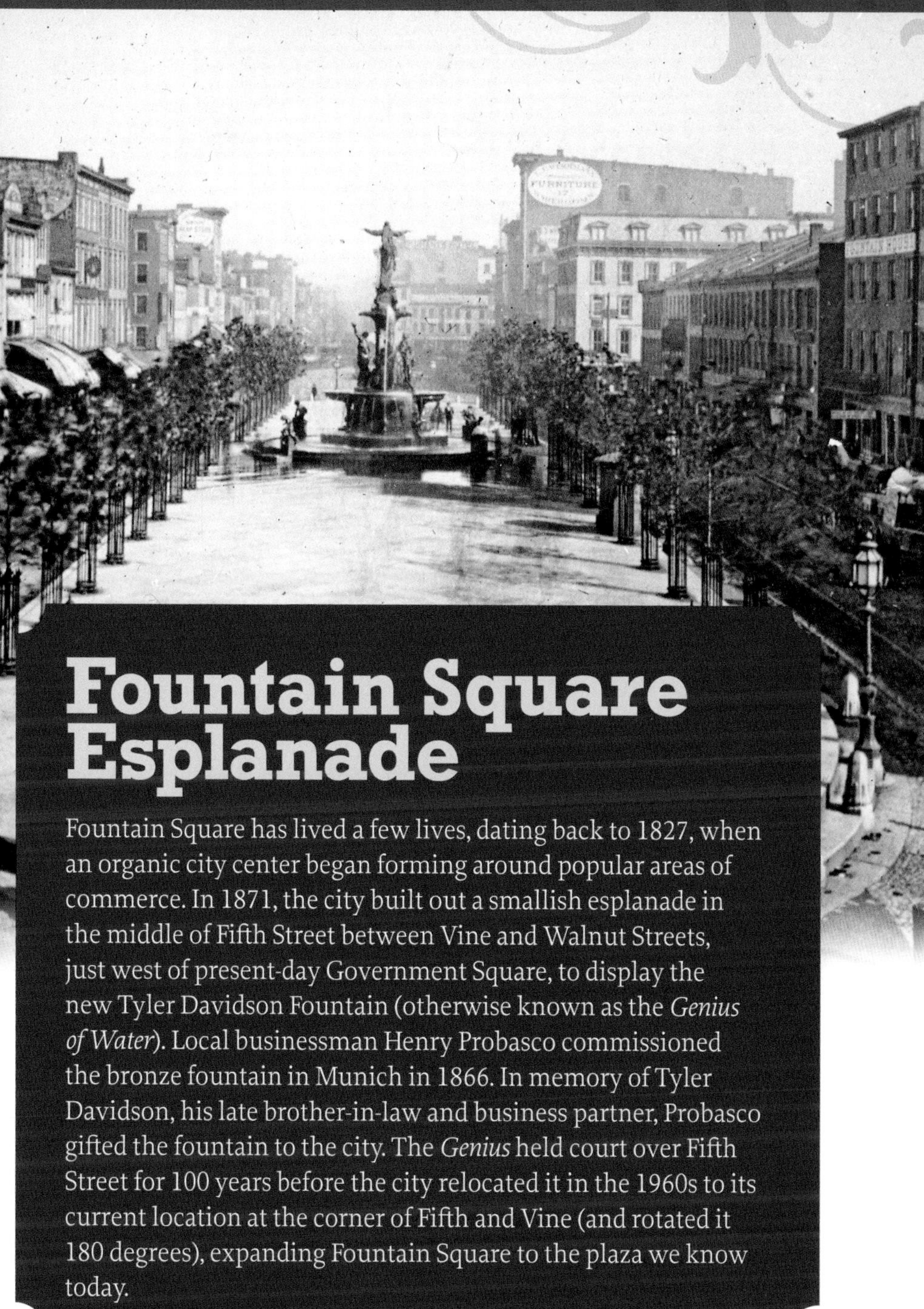

Fountain Square Esplanade

Fountain Square has lived a few lives, dating back to 1827, when an organic city center began forming around popular areas of commerce. In 1871, the city built out a smallish esplanade in the middle of Fifth Street between Vine and Walnut Streets, just west of present-day Government Square, to display the new Tyler Davidson Fountain (otherwise known as the *Genius of Water*). Local businessman Henry Probasco commissioned the bronze fountain in Munich in 1866. In memory of Tyler Davidson, his late brother-in-law and business partner, Probasco gifted the fountain to the city. The *Genius* held court over Fifth Street for 100 years before the city relocated it in the 1960s to its current location at the corner of Fifth and Vine (and rotated it 180 degrees), expanding Fountain Square to the plaza we know today.

Courtesy of the Collection of Cincinnati & Hamilton County Public Library

Miami Building

Little is known about the "Miami Building," except that it was a prominent and attractive part of western downtown's skyscape for more than 70 years. Built in the 1890s on the northwest corner of Fifth and Elm Streets, the eight-story building was torn down in 1964. Just a few years later, the site was the Convention-Exposition Center (which eventually expanded and was renamed the Duke Energy Convention Center) and that corner of western downtown was forever altered.

The Blymer Building

Built in the 1880s on the 500 block of Main Street in a pseudo-Romanesque Revival style, the elaborate Blymer Building was eventually demolished in 1955. It was replaced with the limestone and glass John Weld Peck Federal Building, which was built in 1964 and adorned with a 21-foot aluminum eagle sculpture by artist Marshall Maynard Fredericks (and decorated inside with a Charley Harper mosaic mural).

Pickering Building

None other than Harry Houdini put the otherwise nondescript, lowrise Pickering Building on the map. In 1916, the superstar Hungarian-American magician, known for touring the world and performing fantastic escape tricks, agreed to be confined to a straitjacket and hung upside down by his feet from the top of the Pickering Building on Fifth and Main Streets downtown. (Spoiler alert: He escaped.) Despite this brush with fame, the Pickering Building fell victim to a street-widening project when the city expanded Fifth Street in 1931, and was demolished.

Courtesy of the Collection of Cincinnati & Hamilton County Public Library

Courtesy of the Collection of Cincinnati & Hamilton County Public Library

Custom House and Post Office

You expect to see a building of this magnitude along the River Seine, and indeed, the elaborate structure was designed in the French Second Empire style in 1874 by Alfred B. Mullett (who is best known for designing the iconic State, War, and Navy Building in Washington, DC, now known as the Eisenhower Executive Office Building). The massive Custom House and Post Office was built in response to a need for consolidated Federal office space, and served that purpose until its demolition in 1936. The city did a stylistic about-face with its replacement: a monumental limestone-faced building with a neo-Grecian style now known as the Potter Stewart Courthouse, built in 1939. Still in public use, the building houses the Federal District Courts, including the Sixth Circuit Court of Appeals.

Chamber of Commerce Building

Completed in 1889 at the corner of Fourth and Vine Streets, the Chamber of Commerce building was a study in municipal fabulosity, with "Pink Milford" Worcester granite walls, arched windows stretching three stories up, and steep, red tile corner towers. Though the building was deemed "fireproof" by its own architect, Henry Hobson Richardson (the "Richardson Romanesque" style), it burned all the way down in 1911 due to a grease fire. You can still see its salvaged carved stone eagles, which now grace Eden Park Drive's Melan Arch Bridge.

Old Main Library

The main branch of the Public Library of Cincinnati and Hamilton County is going strong with a brawny mid-century building stretching across two downtown blocks. But the original that it replaced was an unforgettable stunner from an altogether different age. Built in 1870 at 629 Vine Street downtown, the Old Main Library had soaring cast-iron book stacks, spiral staircases, and huge windows that bathed the checkerboard tile floor in natural light. But as post-war libraries looked to expand, the Old Main was too cramped and run down for modern tastes. The building was razed in 1955 and replaced later that year with its sprawling successor.

Images courtesy of the Collection of Cincinnati & Hamilton County Public Library

CHURCHES AND HOUSES OF WORSHIP

Cincinnati has a richer-than-average religious history: Some of its first structures were Christian churches, as founding settlers sought to build a spiritual life in their new home. Late 19th century German immigrants built scores of Catholic churches throughout Cincinnati and Northern Kentucky, many of which continue to thrive. Cincinnati is also the birthplace of American Reform Judaism, established in 1875 with the construction of Hebrew Union College, which calls itself "the first permanent Jewish institution of higher learning in the New World." And downtown's northwest corner is a thicket of spires and towers from different traditions: The Cathedral Basilica of St. Peter in Chains and the Isaac M. Wise Temple have stood side by side for more than 150 years.

Though beloved when built, many of these houses of worship are lost to us, consolidated with other communities or else overtaken by commercial or civic development.

Wesley Chapel

When Wesley Chapel was torn down as a part of Procter & Gamble's downtown expansion, it was the oldest surviving house of worship in Cincinnati. Built in 1831 on East Fifth Street between Broadway and Sycamore Streets, the simple red brick Methodist church was remarkably spacious for the time, with seating for 1,200 (making it the city's largest building for much of its early history). Ten years after its construction, it hosted the funeral of President William Henry Harrison. A nearly 10-year fight with preservationists and P&G ended with the chapel's demolition in 1972. It was more than 140 years old.

LINCOLN PARK BAPTIST CHURCH

Built in 1896 across from the former Lincoln Park at the then corner of Freeman Avenue and Betts Street, the Lincoln Park Baptist Church was a prominent West End landmark, with its domed tower rising over the lush landscaping of the park. The church dates back to 1842, when its founders started meeting in an old saw mill on what is now Sargent Street, near the Ohio River. Along with its namesake park, the church was demolished to make way for the early 1930s construction of Union Terminal.

Courtesy of the Collection of Cincinnati & Hamilton County Public Library

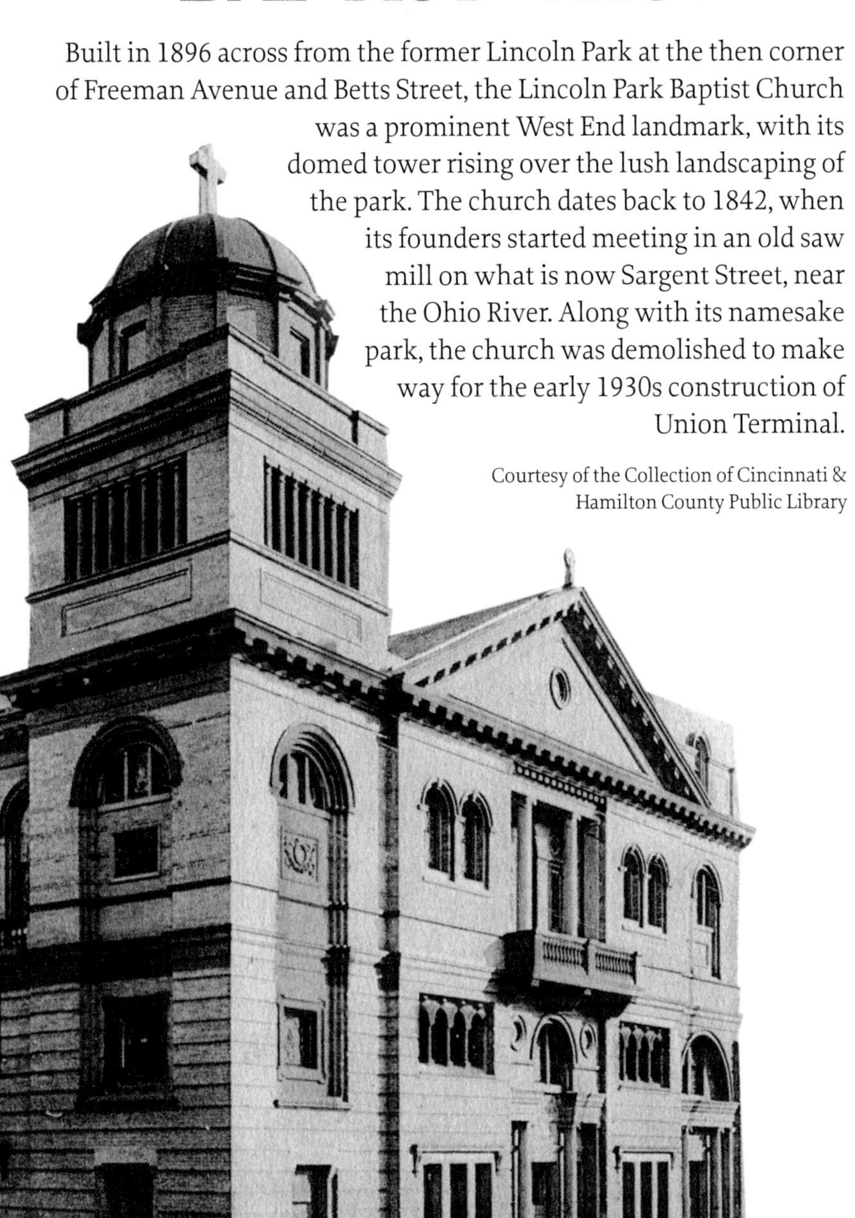

Allen Temple

Allen Temple was built in 1852 as a Bene Israel congregation. In 1866, after the construction of Plum Street Temple, the historic synagogue that is the seat of American Reform Judaism, Allen became the home of the African Methodist Episcopal Church. Itself dating all the way back to 1824, AME was started by Reverend James King (formerly an enslaved man) and Reverend Phillip Brodie. But that layered history didn't protect it from the same corporate expansion that took out dozens of homes, churches, and other buildings sitting in the way of Procter & Gamble's downtown footprint. The Temple building was demolished in 1972, and the Allen Temple AME congregation moved to Roselawn, where it remains today.

Courtesy of Wikimedia

Chapel of the Holy Spirit

This Roman Catholic church was a neighbor on East Fifth Street to the Fenwick Club, both casualties of Procter & Gamble's push to expand its headquarters (along with Allen Temple and Wesley Chapel). Designed by local architect Edward J. Schulte and dedicated in 1927, the Chapel of the Holy Spirit featured a limestone facade over a red brick structure, plus an ornately carved wooden door and stone and copper turret. Despite its beautiful design, efforts to move Holy Spirit to another home in the city never got enough traction, and the church was demolished in 1979.

Courtesy of Gregg Fraley

First Presbyterian Church

Cincinnati's First Presbyterian Church dates to the city's founding, when Israel Ludlow included space for it in his 1789 plan. A clapboard structure was built, which was eventually upgraded in 1830 and again replaced in 1851 with an imposing neo-Gothic stunner worthy of the emerging metropolis around it. Built on the north side of Fourth Street near Main, the church was known for its 280-foot spire towering over the city's financial district. A second church was built on Elm Street (which still stands and operates). The first church, whose upkeep had become prohibitively expensive, was demolished in 1936. The Cincinnati branch of the Federal Reserve Bank now sits on the site.

Courtesy of the Collection of Cincinnati & Hamilton County Public Library

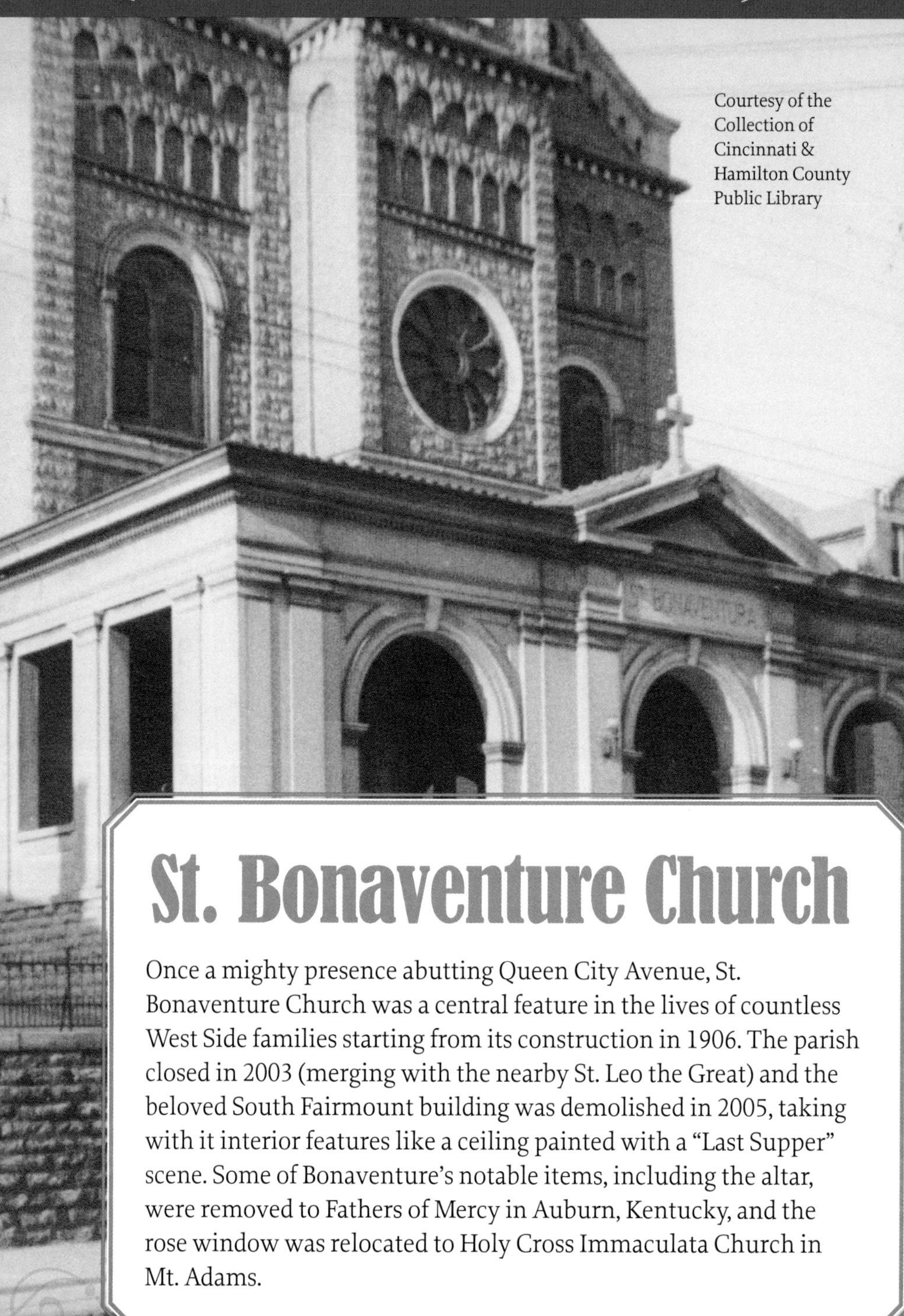

Courtesy of the Collection of Cincinnati & Hamilton County Public Library

St. Bonaventure Church

Once a mighty presence abutting Queen City Avenue, St. Bonaventure Church was a central feature in the lives of countless West Side families starting from its construction in 1906. The parish closed in 2003 (merging with the nearby St. Leo the Great) and the beloved South Fairmount building was demolished in 2005, taking with it interior features like a ceiling painted with a "Last Supper" scene. Some of Bonaventure's notable items, including the altar, were removed to Fathers of Mercy in Auburn, Kentucky, and the rose window was relocated to Holy Cross Immaculata Church in Mt. Adams.

CLUBS AND RESIDENCES

One marker of a liveable city is ready access to rest: Where can you go to relax or recharge? What is your "third place"—that is, your place that is neither home nor work, where you can do exactly what you want or need to do? "Good" cities have these places in spades.

From rest homes to members'-only clubs, these buildings and organizations provided shelter, community, recreation, and comfort. Some operated as safety nets, protecting their residents from the harsh realities of urban life. Other places like the Gamble House, a private home that was otherwise closed to the surrounding neighborhood, gave people a sense of shared history—a landmark around which they would build their own lives.

Images courtesy of Gregg Fraley

Courtesy of Gregg Fraley

Fenwick Club

The Fenwick Club was a catholic alternative to the YMCA, with a residence, library, gym, pool, basketball and handball courts, and a boys' program that kept kids busy and active on winter Saturdays. "I basically grew up there," says Gregg Fraley, whose father Dick worked at Fenwick as the Athletic Director. Founded in 1915, Fenwick hosted social programs and events, and evolved into a downtown institution. Despite its annex building being added to the National Register of Historic Places in 1973, Fenwick was demolished in 1979 (along with the Chapel of the Holy Spirit and a block of other buildings) to make way for neighbor Procter & Gamble's wisteria-crowned courtyard.

The Cincinnati Deutsches Altenheim

The Cincinnati Deutsches Altenheim—otherwise known as the German Home for Old Men—was built in 1893 at 3241 Burnet Street, an address that is now a sea of office buildings and parking garages supporting the University of Cincinnati College of Medicine and Cincinnati Children's Hospital Medical Center. German pioneers had helped to build the region starting in the early 19th century, and the population fairly exploded after the 1830s, building up much of the city that we know today. Cincinnati Children's took over the property in the 1960s and the Altenheim housed residents as late as the 1970s before it was finally demolished.

Courtesy of the Collection of Cincinnati & Hamilton County Public Library

Gamble House

It was a long fight between preservation activists and would-be developers, but the Gamble House in Westwood was finally demolished in 2013. The 13-room Queen Anne-style mansion was occupied by James N. Gamble (son of P&G founder James Gamble) from 1875 until his death in 1932, and had been vacant since 1964. West Side residents mourned the loss, but recent news has it that the former home's 22-acre parcel is slated to become a public park.

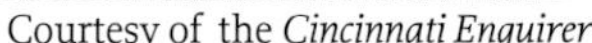

Courtesy of the *Cincinnati Enquirer*

Friars' Club

In 1860, Father Archangelus Gstir of Saint Francis Seraph Church started a program to keep Over-the-Rhine's German youth safe and productively occupied. In 1931, the Friars' Club moved to a new building at the corner of Ohio Avenue and McMillan Street in Clifton Heights, adding a larger gym and swimming pool, a bowling alley (replaced with a ballroom in 1956), and a residency program for male University of Cincinnati students. The fortress-like building became a neighborhood landmark and community gathering place. It was closed in 2005 and demolished in 2010, and the Friars' Club moved to a new facility next to Roger Bacon High School, where it remains.

Courtesy of the Collection of Cincinnati & Hamilton County Public Library

Odd Fellows Temple

The Independent Order of Odd Fellows (IOOF) was a kind of proto Social Security insurance/workers' compensation group, offering benefits for sick leave, funeral expenses, widow/orphan care, and other types of financial relief to its members. The organization was no minor player: IOFF members in Ohio alone were nearly 90,000 strong (both men and women could join). Its immense Hannaford-designed Temple building—seven stories spread over the northwest corner of Seventh and Elm Streets—was dedicated in 1894, and was home to meetings, dances, banquets, and other community gatherings. It was razed in the 1940s to make way for the new Shillito's parking garage.

Anna Louise Inn

Though still operational in its new facility on Reading Road in Mt. Auburn, the Anna Louise Inn once held prime real estate in downtown Cincinnati's Lytle Park, just west of the Taft Museum of Art. Its neo-Georgian building was constructed in 1909 with funds donated by Charles and Anna Taft (and named for their daughter) to provide affordable and safe housing for single women working in the city. It did just that for more than 100 years until 2013, when the Western & Southern Financial Group acquired the building with plans to develop it and the surrounding property into a luxury hotel. Anna Louise Inn moved uptown and took with it a legacy of progressive civic philanthropy in the city center.

Courtesy of the Collection of Cincinnati & Hamilton County Public Library

HOSPITALS

Cincinnati is a "hospital town," boasting some of the finest institutions in the country—namely Cincinnati Children's Hospital Medical Center, which is consistently ranked among the country's best. Since our city's earliest days, residents have been organizing formal treatment centers, from maternity wards to sanitariums, many of which laid the foundation for today's thriving medical systems.

Dunham Hospital

Originally organized in 1816 as an Isolation Hospital or "pest house" for patients suffering from highly communicable diseases—namely smallpox—Dunham Hospital existed throughout downtown and greater Cincinnati in a series of iterations, including on the site currently housing Music Hall, according to the University of Cincinnati Libraries. In 1879, trustees purchased 53 acres in Green Township and renovated an existing farmhouse as a sanitarium, further expanding over the next 10 years, ending up with room for about 450 patients. A cure for tuberculosis was discovered in the 1940s, and Dunham finally closed in 1971. The site now houses the Dunham Recreational Complex.

Bethesda Hospital

Courtesy of the Collection of Cincinnati & Hamilton County Public Library

Bethesda Hospital began its life in a private home in Avondale in 1896, established by Methodist Episcopal Church minister Dr. Christian Golder, who founded Cincinnati's German Methodist Deaconess Association. Just two years later, the hospital moved into a 20-bed building in Mt. Auburn at the corner of Reading Road and Oak Street. As the hospital expanded, it relocated to a new facility in Montgomery in 1970, where it remains. The Mt. Auburn site is now home to the American Cancer Society's Hope Lodge, a residential treatment center for patients and families.

Old Good Samaritan Hospital

Sponsored by the Sisters of Charity and opened in 1852, Good Samaritan Hospital is the longest-running hospital in Cincinnati. The original 21-bed building provided care for locals in need, regardless of their ability to pay. (It was then known as St. John's Hotel for Invalids.) As the institution grew, it changed its name to St. John's Hospital and relocated to Third and Plum Streets, where it played a significant role in caring for Civil War soldiers. In 1915, the hospital moved to Clifton, where it is currently located.

Courtesy of Wikimedia

Booth Memorial Hospital

The building that housed the William Booth Memorial Hospital was originally built in 1869 as a residence for Amos Shinkle on Covington's tony Second Street, just steps from the Ohio River's south banks. When it was converted to a hospital and dedicated in 1926, it was named for William Booth, the founder of the Salvation Army. Additions to the building were made as late as the 1950s; a 1966 postcard lists the bed capacity at "150 and 17 bassinets." The structure has since been refitted as an apartment complex; the original colonnade still stands, inscribed with "Wm. Booth Memorial Hospital."

St. Mary's Hospital

Also known as Betts Street Hospital, St. Mary's was located on Betts Street at Linn Street in the West End (an intersection that no longer exists by that name). The four-story hospital was established in 1859 by the Sisters of the Poor of St. Francis. It was enlarged multiple times through the end of the 19th century, and eventually its imposing brick structure took over the whole corner. St. Mary's treated many thousands of Cincinnatians until it was replaced by the Franciscan (now Mercy Hospital), located in Mt. Airy, in 1971.

Courtesy of Amy Brownlee

ICONS AND CURIOSITIES

Pep Golden Studios

A 1928 advertisement for Pep Golden Studios promised "The Latest Steps as being done in New York Night Clubs and Ball Rooms" (a 16-lesson course in "social dancing" would set you back $20), plus acrobatics, music lessons, and even elocution. Located all around central Cincinnati, from downtown to Avondale, the studios hosted adults' and kids' classes for aspiring nightclubbers and child film stars, respectively. If you were forced into ballroom dancing as a kid in 20th-century Cincinnati, you were very likely at a Pep Golden Studios. And with a compelling precedent, too: Pep Golden's most famous alum was Doris Day, who danced there as a kindergartener.

Courtesy of the Collection of Cincinnati & Hamilton County Public Library

Theda Bara House

Before she was silent film vamp Theda Bara, she was Theodosia Goodman, a tailor's daughter born in Cincinnati, Ohio, in 1895. She attended both Walnut Hills High School and the University of Cincinnati's Cincinnati College of Music. After she hit the big time, Bara built a white stucco villa (modeled after the Spanish villas of her adopted Hollywood home) in the 1920s in her old neighborhood of North Avondale. Xavier University acquired the building in 1979, first using it as housing for nuns and then as the Honors Villa until it was demolished by the university in July 2011.

Courtesy of Getty Images

Courtesy of the University Archives and Special Collections, Xavier University Library, Cincinnati, Ohio

Martha
The Passenger Pigeon

Martha, the Last Passenger Pigeon © 2013 ArtWorks / Design by John A. Ruthven / Location: 15 E. Eighth St. Cincinnati, OH 45202 / Photo by J. Miles Wol

Her death was the end of an era. On September 1, 1914, Martha the Passenger Pigeon, the last remaining of her species, died at the Cincinnati Zoo & Botanical Garden. Passenger pigeons once numbered in the billions in the United States, but deforestation and hunting drove them to extinction. An 1875 Japanese pagoda at the Zoo (one of the early aviary buildings) is now a memorial to Martha. You can also see her and her flock memorialized in mural form by wildlife artist and conservationist John Ruthven at 15 E. Eighth Street, downtown.

Courtesy of Amy Brownlee

Mrs. Trollope's Bazaar

Mrs. Fanny Trollope visited Cincinnati in 1827, and she was not impressed. Her caustic travelog *Domestic Manners of the Americans* describes our town as dull, unbeautiful, riddled with too-proud ladies' maids, and filled with herds of pigs eating garbage in the streets (that last part was true). But it was in Cincinnati that Trollope (the mother of *Vanity Fair* author Anthony Trollope) launched her ambitious business venture: a fantastic Bazaar on Third Street, designed with a ballroom and 40-by-100-foot "Moorish-Arabesque" dome to enhance Cincinnati's then-humble skyline. But it was stocked with junky Euro-style imports that locals didn't want, soon failed, and the Bazaar was torn down in 1881.

Cincinnati Opera at the Cincinnati Zoo

In a happy bit of civic matchmaking, the country's second-oldest opera company premiered in the country's fifth-oldest zoo—and then stuck around for a generation. From its founding season in June 1920, the Cincinnati Opera performances were held at the Cincinnati Zoo Pavilion to wide popularity and acclaim. The Opera spent 50 years there before the permanent move to the Music /hall in 1972. (The Pavilion was razed that same year.) Though the Opera enjoys its indoor digs, Zoo visitors fondly remember the days when the Zoo's elephants would join the *prima donna* on her high notes.

Courtesy of Wikimedia

The Skywalk

Love it or hate it, the Skywalk was an experience. Built in stages from 1972 through 1986, it was meant to bring more foot traffic into the Central Business District while simultaneously freeing the streets for cars (and connecting important structures downtown). Most of its 1.3 miles of elevated walkways were fully enclosed, air-conditioned, and offered clear views of the streets below; it even developed its own retail and restaurant scene. But the Skywalk soon felt dated and underused, with sections falling into disuse and disrepair. And its original mission of enhancing downtown's walking culture failed as it merely poached pedestrians from the streets below. The city turned on the Skywalk as fast as it had adopted it, and removed the last portions in 2020.

Courtesy of the Collection of Cincinnati & Hamilton County Public Library

HERE'S AN AERIAL VIEW of the Convention Way Skywalk. Race Street is below and that's Roy Rogers in the center.

Skywalks Lifting Shoppers Above The Hustle, Bustle

WKRP in Cincinnati

Premiering on CBS in September 1978, *WKRP in Cincinnati* was not actually filmed in Cincinnati. But the opening credits featured a jazzy Cincinnati-themed jingle and a b-roll Valentine that introduced iconic downtown landmarks like the Tyler Davidson Fountain and Carew Tower to a national audience. The show featured the zany misadventures of a fictional local radio station. After four years and 90 episodes, *WKRP* was canceled amid lagging ratings in April 1982. The hilariously dark "Turkeys Away" Thanksgiving episode will go down in sitcom history.

The Kahn's Meat Clock

You gotta have a gimmick. Cincinnati's "Porkopolis" status had diminished somewhat by the time Kahn's dubbed itself "The wiener the world awaited." But it was around this time, after World War II, that Kahn's famous "Meat Clock" appeared at Fifth and Vine as the brand doubled down on our collective post-war appetites. Founded in 1883 by Elias Kahn, the company was instrumental in putting Cincinnati on the pork-producing map. Kahn's was a hometown favorite for everything from BBQs to ballgames. Kahn's was sold to Consolidated Foods Corporation (now Sara Lee) in 1966, and the original 17-acre Camp Washington processing plant shut down in 2006. The "Meat Clock" was lost to the sands of time.

Courtesy of Wikimedia

George Remus Mansion

The house was almost as infamous as the murder. Notorious Prohibition-era lawyer George Remus made his millions running whiskey through secret distilleries all over town. He and his wife, Imogene, hosted legendary parties at their Price Hill showplace where they sent their guests home with diamonds and cars as favors. When Remus was sent to prison in 1925, Imogene promptly filed for divorce and even hired a hitman, who then betrayed her to her husband, who sought his own revenge. In 1927, Remus shot Imogene dead in broad daylight in front of horrified witnesses near Eden Park's Spring House gazebo. He got away with it: Remus pleaded temporary insanity and was acquitted. Their party palace was demolished in 1934 and with it Cincinnati's brush with bootlegging fame.

Courtesy of the *Cincinnati Enquirer*

Courtesy of the Collection of Cincinnati & Hamilton County Public Library

INDUSTRY

Twenty-first century Cincinnati is known for consumer goods powerhouse Procter & Gamble, which has been turning out legacy brands like Tide, Pampers, and Gillette since it floated its first bar of Ivory Soap in 1879. But the city was built on its manufacturing prowess, its citizens making everything from pianos to beer to wrist watches to pottery. Factories around the city and surrounding neighborhoods employed generations of locals and sent Cincinnati-made products around the world.

American Book Company

Best known as the publisher of *McGuffey Readers* (see their entry in Lost Print Media), American Book Company was founded in 1834 (a different company of the same name is headquartered in Georgia) and published educational textbooks and other materials for schools. It changed ownership many times, starting in the 1960s, until its eventual sale to Houghton Mifflin in the 1990s. The company's attractive brick and terra cotta office and factory buildings, built in 1904, were adapted for alternate corporate use in the 1980s; they still stand downtown at the corner of Pike and Third Streets next door to the Taft Museum of Art.

[Eclectic School Series.]

THE

ECLECTIC FIRST READER

FOR

YOUNG CHILDREN,

WITH PICTURES.

BY WILLIAM H. McGUFFEY

PROFESSOR IN MIAMI UNIVERSITY, OXFORD.

—1836—

CINCINNATI:

PUBLISHED BY TRUMAN AND SMITH,

150 MAIN-STREET

Courtesy of McGuffey House and Museum, Miami University

Cincinnati Milling Machine Company

Cincinnati Milling Machine Company began its life in 1874 as Cincinnati Screw and Tap Company, changing its name after an 1889 corporate spinoff. The company soon became a local manufacturing giant, moving to the then new neighborhood of Oakley in 1905. After decades of prominence in machine tooling (punctuated by a major role in two world wars), the Cincinnati Milling Machine Company was dissolved in 1970 and renamed Milacron; it remains a global leader in plastics technology.

Images courtesy of the Collection of Cincinnati & Hamilton County Public Library

Cincinnati Type Foundry

Established in 1826, the Cincinnati Type Foundry had small but important roles in the fields of typography and printing. In 1892, the American Type Founders trust was created by merging 23 different type foundries from around the country, including the Cincinnati Type Foundry, which was well known at the time for having created a portable "Army Press" for the Union during the Civil War. American Type Founders went on to create many industry improvements. The Great Depression began its slow decline and the company finally sold the last of its assets in the 1990s. But Cincinnati's inclusion in this business trust helped to standardize type, document design, and printing around the country.

This local furniture manufacturer was best known for its Barrister bookcases (a four-row case with hinged horizontal glass fronts), which the company called "elastic" because they were fully customizable to individual libraries. It was modular design decades before the likes of Ikea. Globe-Wernicke was founded in 1899, and its plants on Eighth Street downtown and on Norwood's Carthage Avenue produced high-end office furniture up to World War II, when it converted to military production.

In 1955, City Auto Stamping Company (out of Toledo, Ohio) acquired Globe-Wernicke and the company's name became defunct. Those "elastic" cases are now a valuable collector's item.

Courtesy of the Collection of Cincinnati & Hamilton County Public Library

Kenner Toys

Established in 1946, Kenner Toys—named for the location of its corporate offices on Kenner Street just north of Union Terminal in Queensgate—gave us such iconic American toys as the Easy Bake Oven, Play-Doh, and Stretch Armstrong, all developed right here in Cincinnati. Competitor Hasbro, Inc. took ownership of Kenner in the early 1990s, eventually shuttering the local company in 2000. Now a vibrant ArtWorks mural ("Cincinnati's Toy Heritage") at 23 West Court Street downtown offers a small glimpse of Kenner's legacy.

Courtesy of Cincinnati Toy Heritage 2016 ArtWorks Design by Jonathan Queen
Location 23 West Court Street Cincinnati, OH 45202 Photo by J. Miles Wolf

Hudepohl Smokestack

It had been out of commission for nearly 30 years, but the Hudepohl smokestack was still a prominent part of the Queensgate skyline when it met its demise. Clocking in at 170 feet tall, the red brick tower with white lettering was a physical reminder of our city's brewing history, topping the abandoned Hudepohl Brewery building. (That brand was established in 1885.) It was demolished in 2019, but Hudepohl beer has been brought back to life by the Christian Moerlein Brewing Company.

R. K. LeBlond Machine Tool Company

From its founding in 1887, LeBlond Machine Tool Company was a strong manufacturing presence in Cincinnati, exemplified by its factory smokestack rising over Norwood from 1918 until 1989. Known worldwide for producing machine tools (namely metal-turning lathes), LeBlond's attractive facility was the product of an architectural style focusing on aesthetics as much as utility. It was mostly demolished after an acquisition by Makino and a move to Mason, but you can still enjoy much of the site's original charm: The more than 20-acre property is now the Rookwood Pavilion and Rookwood Commons shopping centers, converted in 1993 and 2000, respectively.

Courtesy of Amy Brownlee

Courtesy of the Collection of Cincinnati & Hamilton County Public Library

Gruen Watch Company

In its 60 years in Cincinnati, Gruen Watch Company became one of the largest watch manufacturers in the United States, widely known for high-quality Swiss craftsmanship. (The movements were produced in Switzerland and the cases made and adjusted locally.) Starting in the late 19th-century, Gruen was known for its seemingly countless watch styles at a wide range of price points, including the famous "Curvex" design. In 1917, Gruen moved into "Time Hill" in Mt. Auburn, designed to look like a Medieval guild hall. Though the company dissolved in 1958, the building still stands tall, housing Lighthouse Youth Services.

US PLAYING CARD FACTORY

Once Norwood's most prominent building, the US Playing Card Company factory building and clock tower soared over the neighborhood when it was constructed in 1900. (The four-story tower went up over the building's entrance in 1926.) Hannaford & Sons, of Music Hall fame, designed the 30-acre plan, and the factory produced iconic playing card brands like Bee, Hoyle, Aviator, and Bicycle until the company relocated to Erlanger, Kentucky, in 2009. Most of the building was demolished in 2020 (except a factory wing and that clock tower), and a mixed use development is currently in the works for the land.

Courtesy of the Collection of Cincinnati & Hamilton County Public Library

Baldwin Piano Company

Originally from Erie County, Pennsylvania, D. H. Baldwin opened a retail piano store in Cincinnati in 1862. By the 1890s, the company had achieved international recognition for its concert pianos and by the early 20th century was exporting all over the world as an iconic American brand. In 2001, Gibson Guitar, based in Nashville, acquired Baldwin and then moved its manufacturing to China in 2007. The former Baldwin factory, built in the 1920s at the base of Eden Park and known for its prominent clock tower, is now a handsome apartment building.

Rudolph Wurlitzer & Bro.

When he immigrated to the US in 1853 from Saxony (now part of Germany), Randolph Wurlitzer was on track to become a household name. After settling in Cincinnati, he began importing musical instruments, manufacturing his own after the Civil War. The company was best known for its "Mighty Wurlitzer" theater organ, which accompanied silent films of the time (a 1927 model, built for the RKO Albee Theater, rests now in the Music Hall ballroom). Wurlitzer's rise to prominence lasted well into the 20th century: The company built factories all over the country as recently as 1970. Another local company, Baldwin, bought Wurlitzer in the 1980s, and then Baldwin itself was acquired in 2001 by Nashville's Gibson Guitar Corporation.

Images courtesy of the Collection of Cincinnati & Hamilton County Public Library

Strobridge Lithographing Company

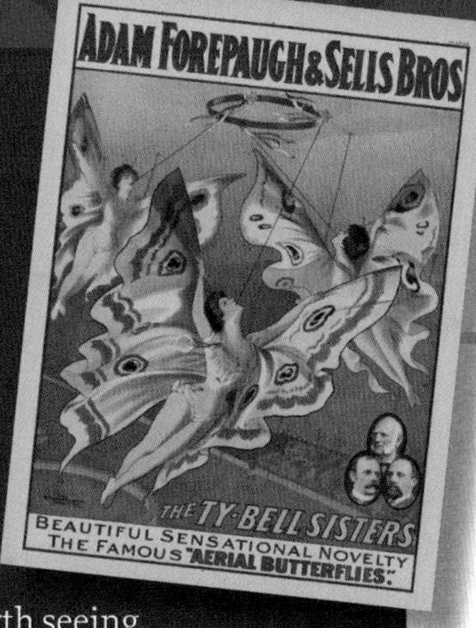

What started as a humble stationery store before the Civil War expanded to a full-scale lithography company producing some of the most vivid media and advertising images in late 19th and early 20th century Cincinnati. If it was worth seeing, Strobridge Lithographing Company promoted it, creating posters advertising everything from stage shows to circus acts. The factory, built in 1884, was situated in Over-the-Rhine along the Miami and Erie Canal. Strobridge's last poster was a 1954 design for Ringling Bros. and Barnum & Bailey Circus.

Crosley Radio Corporation

Powel Crosley Jr. brought affordable radios to the masses with his 1921 "Harko" crystal receiver. In 1924, he began to produce thousands of radios per day from his Samuel Hannaford & Sons-designed factory, rising high in Camp Washington. During this time, Crosley also established 700 WLW, which at 500,000 watts, was the most powerful radio station in the world, broadcasting the Voice of America network globally during World War II. Parent company AVCO stopped producing Crosley radios in 1956 due to declining sales and by the 1970s had sold off the company's manufacturing and broadcast divisions. The factory building still stands, abandoned, but its fate is unresolved (though it was placed on the National Register of Historic Places in 2015).

Images courtesy of the Collection of Cincinnati & Hamilton County Public Library

BREWERIES

No single local industry has had more impact on our collective social life than brewing. German immigrants launched dozens of local breweries in the city in the late 19th and early 20th centuries, and hundreds of bars, taverns, and beer gardens opened to distribute the products locally. Many excellent brands and breweries remain or have launched, including MadTree Brewing and Rhinegeist Brewery. Others also have come back from obscurity, including the Christian Moerlein Brewing Company. As with the rest of the country, Prohibition stopped the party early, and many breweries never recovered.

Images courtesy of the Collection of Cincinnati & Hamilton County Public Library

John Hauck
BREWING COMPANY

When it visited expositions around the country in the late 19th and early 20th centuries, the John Hauck Brewing Company billed itself as "Ohio's Model Brewery," presenting a kinder, gentler brewing company that was ultra-modern and even family-friendly. Brewing at a facility in the West End at the corner of Central Avenue and Dayton Street, Hauck even tried to pitch his beer as a tonic: Ads for "Invalid Bottled Beer" promised that it was "the only remedy for convalescents to gain strength and vitality." Despite its creative marketing, Hauck was mortally wounded by Prohibition, finally closing in 1927.

Red Top Brewing

A well-known post-Prohibition brewery, Red Top began operations in the early 1930s when founders Edgar Mack Sr. and Louis Ullman began brewing beer out of the former Hauck Brewery facility. After World War II, they purchased the former Clyffside brewery and began distributing beer around the country, producing Red Top, Red Top Ale, Twenty Grand Ale, Wunderbrau, and Barbarossa. Sales dropped off in the 1950s, however, and Red Top was sold in 1955 and closed in 1957.

Courtesy of the Collection of Cincinnati & Hamilton County Public Library

Clyffside
Brewing Company

Paul Esselborn opened Clyffside Brewing on McMicken Avenue in 1933, the very year that Prohibition was repealed. The Over-the-Rhine site had been home to other breweries dating all the way back to 1845—namely Hamilton, J.G. Sohn, and Mohawk. Clyffside was short-lived, selling to local Red Top Brewing in 1945, which was itself sold off to a group of investors in 1955. But its Felsenbrau beer and "Brewed in the Hills" Old Hickory Ale are an enduring part of Cincinnati's brewing history.

Images courtesy of the Collection of Cincinnati & Hamilton County Public Library

WINDISCH-MUHLHAUSER BREWING COMPANY

A major local rival to the more famous Christian Moerlein Brewing Company, the Windisch-Muhlhauser Brewing Company was founded in the 1860s by Conrad Windisch (who had helped Moerlein build his empire before starting his own project with Gottlieb Muhlhauser). Windisch-Mulhauser built Lion Brewery on the Miami and Erie Canal (now Central Parkway) at Liberty Street, very near the new TQL Stadium. Prohibition ended Lion's reign, but the brewery campus, part of which you can still see behind the Cincinnati Ballet's training facility, was used to brew Burger beer from 1934-1973.

Crescent Brewing Company

Thomas Gaff founded Crescent Brewing Company in 1853 in Aurora, Indiana. Gaff was a Scottish-born industrialist who nearly single-handedly financed the building of the tri-state town along the Ohio River. (His mansion home, called Hillforest, is a National Historic Landmark.) Crescent Brewery became an international name in brewing and was an integral part of Aurora's growing business community, but it closed down in the 1890s, and most of its buildings were demolished in the 1930s. A new generation, calling itself Great Crescent Brewery, now operates from one of Gaff's original warehouse buildings.

Images courtesy of the Collection of Cincinnati & Hamilton County Public Library

Bavarian BREWING COMPANY

German immigrant Julius Deglow established the Bavarian Brewing Company in Covington, Kentucky, in 1866. The bottling plant, eventually located at 367 Pike Street, was known for its "Riedlin's Select" beer (named for William Riedlin, who later co-owned with John Meyer; Riedlin was known as the proprietor of Over-the-Rhine's Tivoli Hall). Bavarian Brewing was a going concern in Northern Kentucky until well into the 1960s.

Bruckmann Brewing

Frederick Bruckmann started Cumminsville Brewery in present-day Northside in 1856, later partnering with his brother Johan Casper. Johan eventually took over, passing the brewery to his own sons. Bruckmann remained open during Prohibition in part because they sold the brazenly titled "Aristocrat Cereal Beverage" and "Malt Tonic." (In fact, Bruckmann was able to distribute beer to Cincinnati literally moments after Prohibition's repeal, since they never really stopped making it.) Bruckmann stayed in the family until 1949, when it was sold to the Herschel Condon Brewing Company. The brewery closed shortly after, but you can still see its smokestack (now labeled "Worthmore") rising over Central Parkway.

Images courtesy of the Collection of Cincinnati & Hamilton County Public Library

Heidelberg Brewing Company

The name "Heidelberg" is now almost exclusively associated with a large beverage distribution company, but Heidelberg was also a post-Prohibition name in brewing. (The "wholesome" and "healthful" Student Prince Beer was a local favorite.) Just a few years after its founding, however, its Fourth Street facility was severely damaged in the Ohio River flood of 1937, and the brewery never fully recovered.

SCHOENLING BREWING COMPANY

When it opened on Good Friday in 1934, Shoenling was called "Schoenling Brewing and Malting Company." Throughout the next few decades, Schoenling—eventually renamed Schoenling Brewing Company—became one of the city's major 20th-century breweries, billing itself as having "Cincinnati's most modern brewery." It was known to mid-century Cincinnatians alongside such brands as Clyffside Brewing Company and Hudepohl. In fact, in the 1980s, Schoenling merged with Hudepohl and its "Little Kings" brand was revived in the 2000s. So Schoenling is not lost so much as reduced, now part of the Christian Moerlein Brewing Company's expanding portfolio.

Images courtesy of the Collection of Cincinnati & Hamilton County Public Library

CROWN BREWING

You can walk through one of Crown Brewery's old brewery cellars, which is now part of Over-the-Rhine's Brewing Heritage Trail. The pre-Prohibition cellar is 30 feet underground, its cooler air making it possible for brewers to create and store the lager beer they were known for. The Crown Brewery was short-lived—open from 1904–1919—but quickly stood out among the city's dozens of other breweries. The production building at 131 East McMicken Avenue has been repurposed as lofts and office space.

Courtesy of the Collection of Cincinnati & Hamilton County Public Library

NEIGHBORHOODS

The number of neighborhoods in Cincinnati remains a subject for debate. The widely accepted count is 52. But you'll also hear estimates north of 70 as citizens and their leaders seek to include communities in Northern Kentucky and places extending from the city center in the civic tally. What we can all agree upon is that there were once neighborhoods that are either off the map completely—either slowly overtaken by sprawl or forcibly removed by government action—or so fundamentally altered as to be essentially lost.

West End

It took an interstate highway to tear apart the West End. According to Dr. Eric R. Jackson, Professor of History at Northern Kentucky University, about 70 percent of Cincinnati's African-American population lived in the West End by the 1930s (and had lived there in the thousands since before the Civil War). In 1948, Cincinnati City Council adopted a Master Plan that included the eventual construction of Interstate 75, which would plow through the West End, destroying blocks of historic row houses and other buildings. Much of the thriving African-American community who had called that district home for generations was scattered to uptown neighborhoods, and Cincinnati would never be the same.

Kenyon-Barr

It was a densely populated neighborhood of nearly 30,000 people, but the city insisted that it was a blighted slum and so Kenyon-Barr was razed in 1958. A key West End quarter, Kenyon-Barr was also the heart of downtown Cincinnati's black community, and its elimination from the urban landscape was itself a clear moment of cultural displacement and erasure as the city demolished dozens of churches, hundreds of restaurants, and thousands of homes. What remained—multi-lane roads and empty lots—was renamed Queensgate.

Little Africa

According to Carl Westmoreland, senior historian at the National Underground Railroad Freedom Center, this western riverfront neighborhood "was called Little Africa because it was a point of entry for people of African descent who came to Cincinnati." Those people, most of whom had escaped slavery, looked to rebuild their lives in Cincinnati, and founded one of the city's first predominantly black neighborhoods. But they found fierce and often violent competition for food and jobs from the growing Irish immigrant population and other groups. The populations on the riverfront eventually relocated to other neighborhoods further uptown, and "Little Africa" is now known as the Banks.

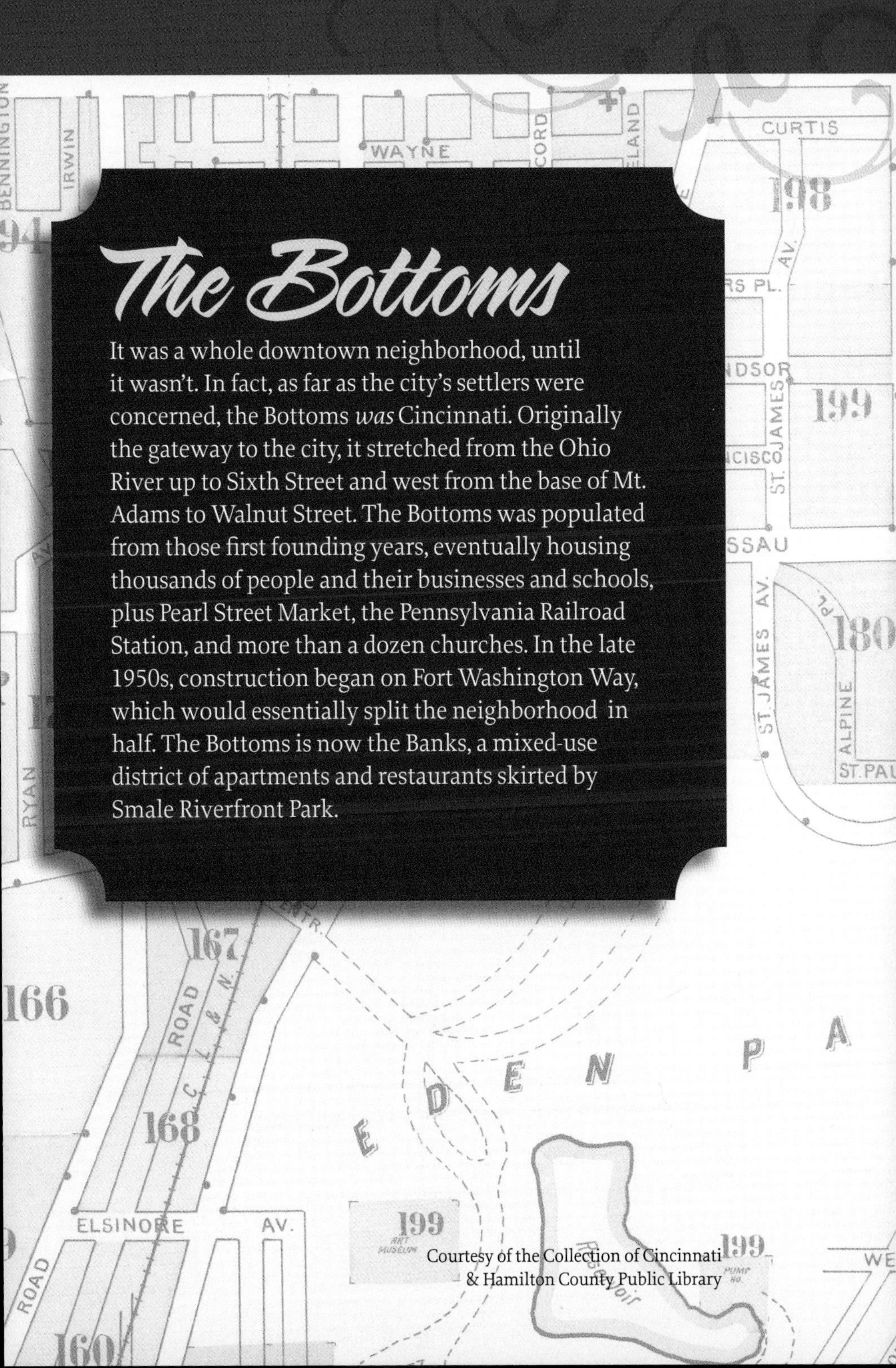

The Bottoms

It was a whole downtown neighborhood, until it wasn't. In fact, as far as the city's settlers were concerned, the Bottoms *was* Cincinnati. Originally the gateway to the city, it stretched from the Ohio River up to Sixth Street and west from the base of Mt. Adams to Walnut Street. The Bottoms was populated from those first founding years, eventually housing thousands of people and their businesses and schools, plus Pearl Street Market, the Pennsylvania Railroad Station, and more than a dozen churches. In the late 1950s, construction began on Fort Washington Way, which would essentially split the neighborhood in half. The Bottoms is now the Banks, a mixed-use district of apartments and restaurants skirted by Smale Riverfront Park.

Courtesy of the Collection of Cincinnati & Hamilton County Public Library

SCHOOLS AND PARKS

Ohio Mechanic's Institute

In 1828, Cincinnati was rapidly becoming a highly industrialized economy, along with much of the rest of the world. That year saw the opening of one of the first technical schools in the country, the Ohio Mechanics Institute. Eventually housed in the Emery Building, built in 1911 and still standing at Walnut and Central Parkway, OMI provided training and other educational opportunities to skilled tradesmen at little to no cost. (Though it did not accept recent immigrants or African-Americans until 1951.) In 1969, OMI (then known as the Ohio College of Applied Science), was incorporated in the University of Cincinnati, becoming the College of Engineering and Applied Science.

Courtesy of the Collection of Cincinnati & Hamilton County Public Library

Columbian School

This 18-room school was built in Avondale between 1893 and 1897 in a burly Richardsonian Romanesque style, and according to the Library of Congress, "represented a major city investment in [that] newly annexed neighborhood." The handsome building was a landmark in the community, serving as the public school setting for countless local students. Columbian School had a hundred-year presence at 3415 Harvey Avenue, at the northeast corner of Martin Luther King Drive, before it was demolished in 1993 and replaced with a surface parking lot.

Ohio Military Institute

The neighborhood of College Hill is so named because a series of schools, including Farmers College, Ohio Female College, and Ohio Military College, were founded there. Originally known as Cary's Academy for Boys, which was established in 1832 on Belmont Avenue, the school eventually underwent a number of name changes; it was renamed Ohio Military Institute in 1890, and it operated as such until 1958. Of note, the school educated President William Henry Harrison and functioned as a stop on the Underground Railroad. True to form, part of the original property now houses Aiken High School.

Courtesy of Wikimedia

FREDERICK DOUGLASS SCHOOL

Reverend Dangerfield Early was leader of the Walnut Hills Baptist Church in 1858 when he founded a school for Cincinnati's African-American children. In 1872, shortly after the city incorporated Walnut Hills, the school was moved into a new building and named Elm Street School. According to the Cincinnati History Library, school officials were up against increasing pressure to integrate following the Civil War. Though the school was technically open admission, its leaders sought instead to maintain a safe and high-quality educational environment for black students, led by black faculty and staff. In 1902, Elm Street School was renamed Frederick Douglass Elementary School (after the famed abolitionist and writer). In 1911, the school moved into a brand new building with 19 classrooms and amenities like a gym and auditorium and even a three-room model apartment (for Home Ec. classes). Although the school moved from its old building in the 1970s, Frederick Douglass School remains a local institution.

Courtesy of the Collection of Cincinnati & Hamilton County Public Library

Courtesy of the Collection of Cincinnati & Hamilton County Public Library

Lincoln Park

One of Cincinnati's first public parks, Lincoln Park was landscaped in the West End in 1858 on a former potter's field (whose remains were relocated). Originally called West End Park, it was renamed after President Lincoln's assassination in 1865. It was a lush property with a manmade lake, grotto, island, and bandstand, and later in 1892, a shelter/refreshments house that hosted thousands of visitors each week. The park was mostly removed and re-graded to make way for Union Terminal, and the site is now that building's parking lot, though some re-landscaped elements remain as the esplanade.

TRANSPORTATION

In the early 20th century, Cincinnatians had more than a few options for getting around town: Passenger train stations were in most major neighborhoods, inclines connected the basin with hilltop amenities, flat-bottomed boats moved freight up and down the Miami and Erie Canal, and steamboats rolled along the Ohio River. All of these are our lost transportation treasures. There were lost opportunities, too: We almost had a subway system, which would have remade the very fabric of the city.

Courtesy of the Collection of Cincinnati & Hamilton County Public Library

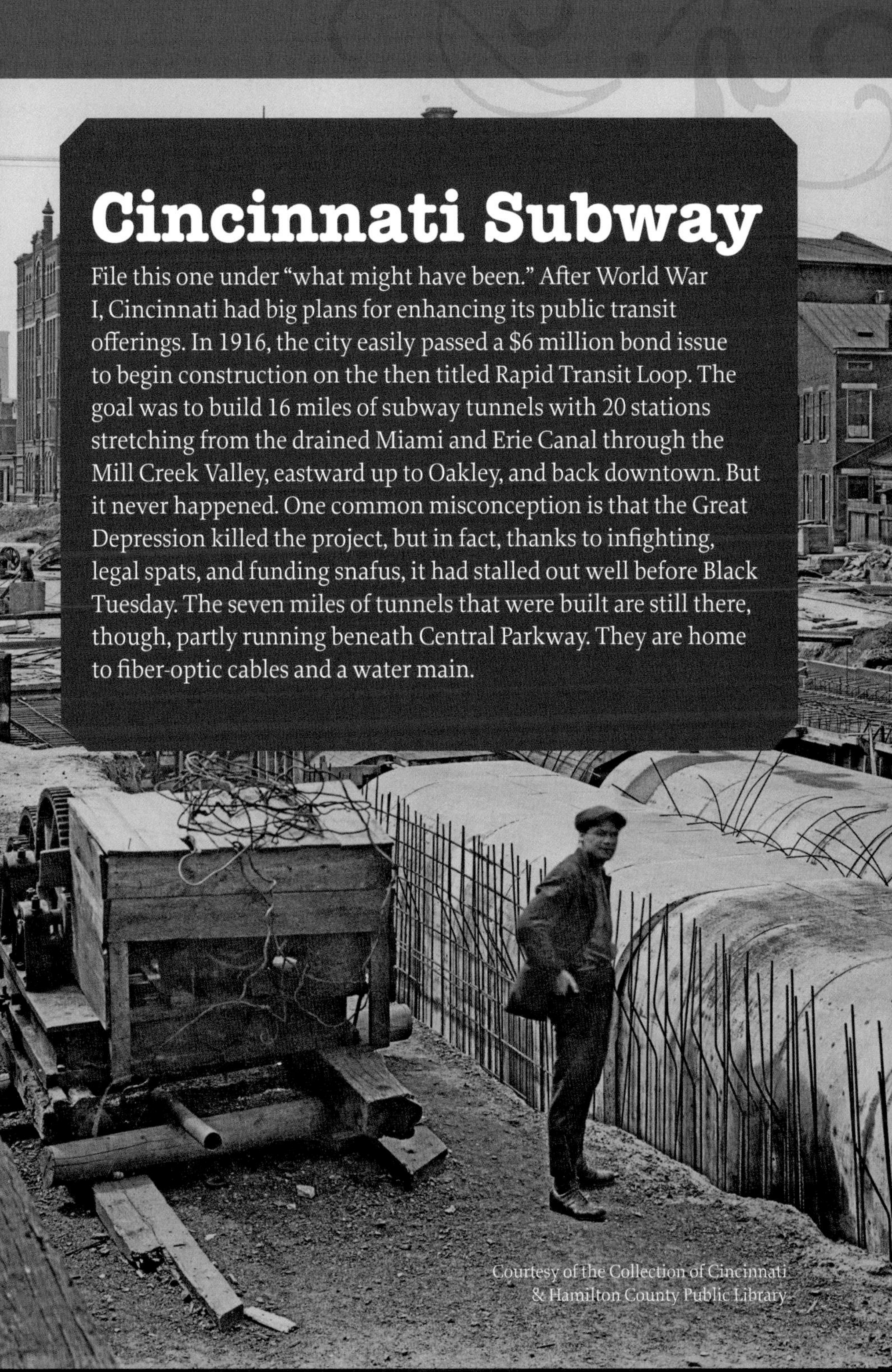

Cincinnati Subway

File this one under "what might have been." After World War I, Cincinnati had big plans for enhancing its public transit offerings. In 1916, the city easily passed a $6 million bond issue to begin construction on the then titled Rapid Transit Loop. The goal was to build 16 miles of subway tunnels with 20 stations stretching from the drained Miami and Erie Canal through the Mill Creek Valley, eastward up to Oakley, and back downtown. But it never happened. One common misconception is that the Great Depression killed the project, but in fact, thanks to infighting, legal spats, and funding snafus, it had stalled out well before Black Tuesday. The seven miles of tunnels that were built are still there, though, partly running beneath Central Parkway. They are home to fiber-optic cables and a water main.

Courtesy of the Collection of Cincinnati & Hamilton County Public Library

Torrence Road Station

Built in 1907 by the Pennsylvania Railroad line, this station sat on the hillside above Riverside Drive (directly across from Saint Rose Church, which was founded in 1867). At its peak, Pennsylvania Station serviced two dozen passenger trains per day. It was demolished in 1933, the same year that Union Terminal opened. It's not completely gone though: Visitors to the site can see the original foundation and, along the tracks above, a huge 25-by-12-foot relief sculpture, which was relocated here from Philadelphia in 1923 after a fire destroyed their original station. Due to its exposure to the elements, it has fallen into disrepair, but it hints at the scale of what once was.

Courtesy of the Collection of Cincinnati & Hamilton County Public Library

Pennsylvania Station

Before the Union Terminal dome rose over the West End, a constellation of train stations dotted Cincinnati neighborhoods, one for each of the region's different railroad companies. But some of these, including the stately Pennsylvania Station located at the corner of Pearl and Butler Streets in the Bottoms, were susceptible to flooding, and local officials moved to centralize train service away from the river. In 1933, most local operations were rerouted to the new terminal, which proved a prescient decision: The Ohio River's most catastrophic flood in the history of the city happened just four years later.

Oakley Train Station

(former Baltimore & Ohio train station)

Built in 1903 to replace the original Marietta & Cincinnati Railroad station that had burned down, the depot later known as the Oakley Train Station was a major stop on the Baltimore & Ohio Railroad. The station received rail passengers up until 1971, after which it was decommissioned, abandoned, and eventually condemned. Despite a long fight from preservationists who cited its role in settling the city neighborhood of Oakley and the surrounding residential area, the station was demolished in July 2013.

Cin., Ham. & Dayton and Dayton & Mich. R. R's.

CINCINNATI TO TOLEDO.

Cincinnati	0
Cuminsville	5
Spring Grove / Winton Place	7
Carthage	10
Lockland	12
Glendale	15
Jones'	19
Hamilton	25
Busenbarck's	31
Trenton	33
Middletown	37
Poast Town	40
Carlisle	44
Miamisburg	49
Carrolton	53
Dayton	60
Tippecanoe	74
Troy	80
Piqua	88
Sidney	100
Anna	107
Wapakoneta	119
Lima	131
Columbus Grove	144
Ottawa	151
Belmore	162
Milton	172
Weston	176
Tontogany	182
Perrysburg	193
Toledo	202

C. H. and D. Station

British engineer-turned-railway baron John Alexander Collins founded C. H. and D.—short for Cincinnati, Hamilton, and Dayton Railway—in 1846; it's just one of dozens of defunct Ohio railroads that claimed rights-of-way and graded rail lines throughout the state during the 19th century. The C. H. and D. station at the corner of Fifth and Wood (now Baymiller) Streets in the West End hosted passenger and freight traffic, and by the Civil War had developed a reputation for being hopelessly congested. After a 1917 acquisition by the Baltimore and Ohio Railroad, the station became known as B. & O. Baymiller Station.

Inset images courtesy of Wikipedia
Background image courtesy Snile, https://commons.wikimedia.org/wiki/File:C_H_and_C_Map_1873.jpg

Central Union Station

Third Street and Central Avenue downtown, now a tangle of interlacing highway ramps, was once the center of rail travel in Cincinnati. Built in 1883, the ornate Central Union Station housed major railroad lines and connected the city to more than 2,000 miles of railways. The position of the building so near the Ohio River, however, turned out to be a major liability, and the city planned a new station in the West End, well away from flood risk. Demolition began in 1933, the year Central Union turned 50 years old and the same year that Union Terminal, its polished replacement, opened.

Courtesy of the Collection of Cincinnati & Hamilton County Public Library

Inclines

In the days before anti-lock brakes, making your way up Cincinnati's steep hillsides was treacherous, prompting most people to live, work, and socialize in the city's level basin. But a series of inclines that carted people up and down the hills helped Cincinnatians to spread out of the city center. Opened in the 1870s, our five inclines—Mt. Adams, Price Hill, Fairview, Bellevue, and Mt. Auburn—ushered in a golden age of public transit. They even hauled up the original streetcars, connecting the central hills to the wide city beyond. The last incline disembarked in 1948 as Cincinnati (along with the rest of the country) entered the Age of the Automobile.

Courtesy of the Collection of Cincinnati & Hamilton County Public Library

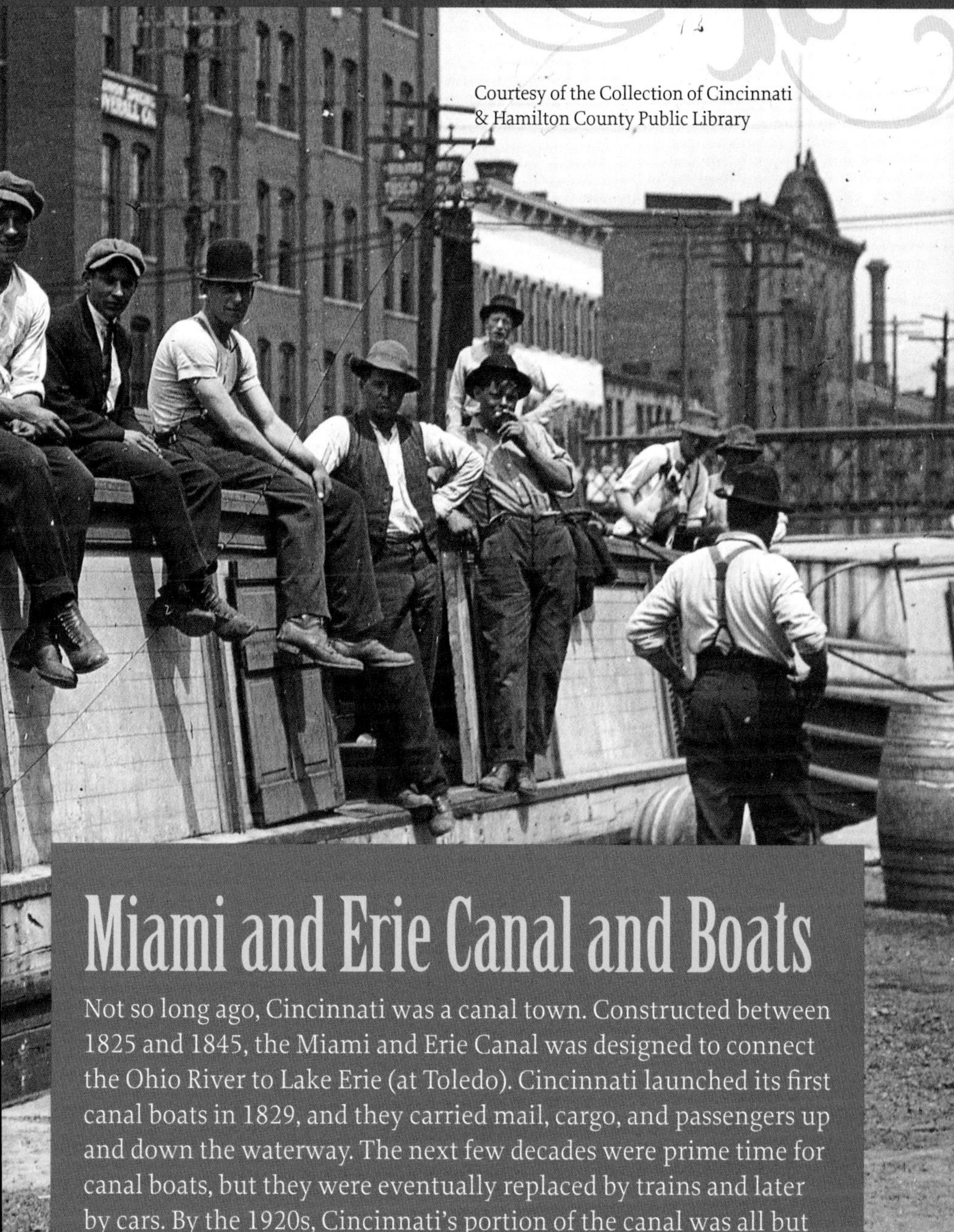
Courtesy of the Collection of Cincinnati & Hamilton County Public Library

Miami and Erie Canal and Boats

Not so long ago, Cincinnati was a canal town. Constructed between 1825 and 1845, the Miami and Erie Canal was designed to connect the Ohio River to Lake Erie (at Toledo). Cincinnati launched its first canal boats in 1829, and they carried mail, cargo, and passengers up and down the waterway. The next few decades were prime time for canal boats, but they were eventually replaced by trains and later by cars. By the 1920s, Cincinnati's portion of the canal was all but abandoned, and it was drained in 1927 and replaced with Central Parkway.

Steamboats

There is perhaps no more romantic Ohio River character than the steamboat. The steam engine made river travel easier than ever before and therefore river towns were much more accessible for living and working. Cargo- and passenger-laden steamboats were a common site on the river for most of the 19th century and well into the 20th century, with names like the *Betsy Ann*, *Island Queen*, *Golden Belle*, *Belle of Calhoun*, and *Valley Belle*. With their glory days long gone, a few steamboats like BB Riverboats are still in operation for pleasure cruises.

Courtesy of the Collection of Cincinnati & Hamilton County Public Library

INDEX